Waste

C000177993

Harley Granville Barker (1877–1946) was the most brilliant British director of the first quarter of the twentieth century. His best-known plays, including *Waste* (banned by the Lord Chamberlain), were written as contributions to his company's repertoire of provocative modern drama for a subsidised national theatre, a cause he championed in his book *A National Theatre: Scheme and Estimates*. *Waste* was first presented by the Stage Society in 1907, revised and produced at the Westminster Theatre, 1936. Other plays include *The Voysey Inheritance*, written 1903–5, first produced at the Court Theatre, 1905, revised version produced at Sadler's Wells Theatre, 1934; *The Madras House*, first produced at the Duke of York's Theatre, 1910, revised 1925 for production at the Ambassadors Theatre; *The Secret Life*, written 1919–22, posthumously produced at the Orange Tree Theatre, Richmond, 1989; and *His Majesty*, written 1923–8, posthumously produced by Orange Tree Theatre Company in 1992 at the St Bride's Centre during the Edinburgh International Festival.

The Voysey Inheritance

PLAYS: ONE
(The Voysey Inheritance, Waste, The Secret Life,
Rococo, Vote by Ballot)

PLAYS: TWO
(The Marrying of Anne Leete, The Madras House,
His Majesty, Farewell to the Theatre)

Harley Granville Barker

Waste

Bloomsbury Methuen Drama
An imprint of Bloomsbury Publishing Plc

BLOOMSBURY
LONDON · OXFORD · NEW YORK · NEW DELHI · SYDNEY

Bloomsbury Methuen Drama
An imprint of Bloomsbury Publishing Plc

50 Bedford Square   1385 Broadway
London   New York
WC1B 3DP   NY 10018
UK   USA

www.bloomsbury.com

Bloomsbury is a registered trademarks of Bloomsbury Publishing Plc

First published in 1909, revised 1926,
and published 1927 by Sidgwick & Jackson Ltd, London
This edition contains the 1926 revised version

Copyright © 1909, 1927 Harley Granville Barker
Copyright © 1936 Harley Granville Barker
Copyright © 1955 Estate of Granville Barker

British Library Cataloguing-in-Publication Data
A catalogue record for this book is available from the British Library

ISBN: PB: 978-1-4742-7739-6
ePub: 978-1-4742-7740-2
ePDF: 978-1-4742-7741-9

Library of Congress Cataloging-in-Publication Data
A catalog record for this book is available from the Library of Congress

Typeset by Country Setting, Kingsdown, Kent CT14 8ES
Printed and bound in Great Britain

The National Theatre is dedicated to making the very best theatre and sharing it with as many people as possible.

We stage up to 30 productions at our South Bank home each year, ranging from re-imagined classics – such as Greek tragedy and Shakespeare – to modern masterpieces and new work by contemporary writers and theatre-makers. The work we make strives to be as open, as diverse, as collaborative and as national as possible. Much of that new work is researched and developed at the NT Studio: we are committed to nurturing innovative work from new writers, directors, creative artists and performers. Equally, we are committed to education, with a wide-ranging Learning programme for all ages in our new Clore Learning Centre and in schools and communities across the UK.

The National's work is also seen on tour throughout the UK and internationally, and in collaborations and co-productions with regional theatres. Popular shows transfer to the West End and occasionally to Broadway; and through the National Theatre Live programme, we broadcast live performances to 2,000 cinemas in 50 countries around the world. Through National Theatre: On Demand in Schools, three acclaimed, curriculum-linked productions are free to stream on demand in every secondary school in the country. Online, the NT offers a rich variety of innovative digital content on every aspect of theatre.

We do all we can to keep ticket prices affordable and to reach a wide audience, and use our public funding to maintain artistic risk-taking, accessibility and diversity.

Waste was first staged at a private performance by the Stage Society at the Imperial Theatre, Westminster, on 24 November 1907, under the direction of the author. The cast was as follows:

Lady Davenport	Amy Coleman
Walter Kent	Vernon Steel
Mrs Farrant	Beryl Faber
Miss Trebell	Henrietta Watson
Mrs O'Connell	Aimée De Burgh
Lucy Davenport	Dorothy Thomas
George Farrant	Frederick Lloyd
Russell Blackborough	A. Holmes-Gore
A Footman	Allan Wade
Henry Trebell	Granville Barker
Simpson	Mary Barton
Gilbert Wedgecroft	Berte Thomas
Lord Charles Cantelupe	Dennis Eadie
The Earl of Horsham	Henry Vibart
Edmunds	Trevor Lowe
Justin O'Connell	J. Fisher White

Waste received its first public performance at the Westminster Theatre, London, on 1 December 1936, in a version (as printed here) revised by the author in 1926. The cast was as follows:

Walter Kent	Stephen Murray
Countess Mortimer	Nina Boucicault
Lady Julia Farrant	Mary Hinton
Frances Trebell	Gillian Scaife
Lucy Davenport	Mary MacOwen
Amy O'Connell	Catherine Lacey
George Farrant	A. Scott-Gatty
Russell Blackborough	Cecil Trouncer
Butler	Robert Dalzell
Henry Trebell	Nicholas Hannen
Bertha	Bridget Phelps
Sir Gilbert Wedgecroft	Harcourt Williams
Lord Charles Cantilupe	Gibb McLaughlin
Cyril Horsham	Felix Aylmer
Vivian Saumarez	Alfred Gray
Justin O'Connell	Mark Dignam

Directed by Harley Granville Barker and Michael MacOwan

This edition of *Waste* has been published to coincide with the National Theatre's revival, which opened on 10 November 2015 with the following cast and creative team:

Walter Kent	Hubert Burton
Countess Mortimer	Doreen Mantle
Lady Julia Farrant	Lucy Robinson
Frances Trebell	Sylvestra Le Touzel
Lucy Davenport	Emerald O'Hanrahan
Amy O'Connell	Olivia Williams
George Farrant	William Chubb
Russell Blackborough	Louis Hilyer
The Butler	Ian Jervis
Henry Trebell	Charles Edwards
Bertha	Fleur Keith
Sir Gilbert Wedgecroft	Andrew Havill
Lord Charles Cantilupe	Gerrard McArthur
Vivian Saumarez	Stephen Rashbrook
Justin O'Connell	Paul Hickey
Cyril Horsham	Michael Elwyn

Understudies
Christopher Birch (Cantilupe/Horsham), Martin Chamberlain (Farrant/O'Connell), Laura Fitzpatrick (Amy/Frances/Bertha), Tom Forrister (Kent/Saumarez/Butler), Ian Jervis (Blackborough/Wedgecroft), Fleur Keith (Lucy Davenport), Stephen Rashbrook (Trebell), Claire Vousden (Lady Julia/ Countess Mortimer)

Director Roger Michell
Designer Hildegard Bechtler
Lighting Designer Rick Fisher
Music Matthew Scott
Sound Designer John Leonard
Movement Director Quinny Sacks
Company Voice Work Richard Ryder
Staff Director Oscar Toeman
Casting Wendy Spon

Waste

Characters

Walter Kent
Lady Mortimer
Lady Julia Farrant
Frances Trebell
Lucy Davenport
Amy O'Connell
George Farrant
Russell Blackborough
Butler
Henry Trebell
Maid
Sir Gilbert Wedgecroft
Lord Charles Cantilupe
Cyril Horsham
Vivian Samaurez
Justin O'Connell
Bertha

The action takes place in England in 1927.

Note

In accordance with Granville Barker's practice, emphasised words and phrases in dialogue are indicated by spaced rather than italic type (e.g., e m p h a s i s e d, not *emphasised*).

Act One

Shapters, which is thirty miles or so from London, is a typically English home. Its kitchens are Tudor; it faces the world looking seventeenth century; from the garden you would call it Queen Anne. But the sanctity of age is upon even this last and not least ruthless of its patchings and scrappings, and the effect of the whole is beautiful.

It is a Sunday evening in summer, and in one of the smaller sitting-rooms **Lady Julia Farrant** *has been playing to some of her weekend guests. She is a woman of fifty; she plays very well for an amateur. She has just launched into Chopin's shortest prelude (Op. 28, No. 20). Her listeners are her mother,* **Lady Mortimer**, *a genuinely old lady and dowered with all the beauty of age;* **Frances Trebell**, *a woman in her fifties who has nothing smart about her, her face showing more thought than feeling;* **Amy O'Connell**, *a charming woman, who takes care she does charm;* **Lucy Davenport**, *a girl in her twenties, more grave than gay; and* **Walter Kent**, *just such a young man as the average English father would wish his son to be. They are all attentive. The room is not so brightly lit but that one can see in the moonlight – for the curtains are drawn back and the long windows are open – a paved garden set in a courtyard of some sort, and lights in the rooms beyond. The room is evidently a woman's room, and its owner's taste, one would guess, was formed in the school of Burne-Jones. Having finished the prelude,* **Lady Julia** *shuts the piano and, after a moment, leaves it.*

Walter Kent   Oh . . . was that 'God Save the King'? I'd have stood up.

Lady Mortimer   Thank you, my dear Julia.

Lady Julia   Thank you for listening, Mamma. That's the polite reply, isn't it?

Frances Trebell   Chopin for a finish, Julia . . . after John Sebastian!

Lady Julia   Allow us that much emotional indulgence.

Walter Kent   Romantic moonrise into a starlit sky.

Lucy Davenport   Fived Frances has lectured on Bagehot.

Frances Trebell   No. Mathematics were my bread and butter.

Amy O'Connell   And Lady Mortimer will tell us that she once saw Bagehot plain. And I'm sure he was plain.

Lady Mortimer   Yes . . . he used to come to my father's house . . . with Mr Richard Hutton . . . when I was small. They had long beards . . . which frightened me.

Amy O'Connell   That's better. Now, Mr Kent . . . what's your contribution?

Walter Kent   I have been lectured on Bagehot . . . and examined on Bagehot. And it never, please Heaven, can happen again.

Lucy Davenport   Shame!

Amy O'Connell   Well . . . if I'd only thought of it I might have put all you clever, well-brought-up people in the shade by protesting loudly at dinner to the distinguished statesmen each side of me that I'd never even heard of Bagehot! Though I have . . . oh yes, in my hot youth, I have!

Lady Julia   Who did bring you up, Amy?

Her tone is ever so slightly tart, as **Mrs O'Connell** *is quick to hear – and she counters.*

Amy O'Connell   Dear Julia . . . there's no scandal about it! I was orphaned at two and bequeathed to a great-uncle, who was a parson and an atheist and too clever for his job and too conceited to ask for a better one. And he thought the whole duty of woman was to be pretty . . .

Lady Mortimer   You gave him no trouble there, my dear.

Amy O'Connell   Kind Lady Mortimer! Pretty and agreeable and helpless. He drank casks of Madeira . . . and that was old-fashioned too . . . and had a dreadful temper.

Frances Trebell   Cause and effect, possibly.

Amy O'Connell I think suppressed atheism was worse for it. So I married at seventeen and turned Catholic and went to Ireland with Justin. Then Justin turned Sinn Fein and I came back . . . and everyone was so kind. And that's enough about me. But if I'd only been sent to Cambridge instead . . . and been lectured at by Frances, perhaps, on mathematics and morals . . . what a very different woman I should be! More like Lucy . . . though never so nice. Or I might have gone in for politics and been a power in the land.

Frances Trebell I don't see you tramping the Lobbies in those pretty shoes.

Amy O'Connell No, no . . . a power behind the throne . . . like Julia. But, of course, never so powerful.

Lady Julia (*a shade wryly; only a shade*) I'm not so powerful, I fear.

Amy O'Connell (*who can be very innocent at times*) Aren't you? Don't you make history? I thought all the diaries that can't possibly be published for Heaven knows how long must be full of you. I thought we were all here this weekend helping you make history. The election coming . . . this horrid, hypocritical Lib-Labour government to be beautifully beaten . . . dear Horsham to be sent for again to save the country . . . with Mr Blackborough to find the money and Mr Trebell to find the brains. And that you were arranging it all, Julia.

Lady Julia I wish the country's salvation were so simple a matter.

This may sound a little smug; but **Lady Julia** *does not like you to chaff her unless she likes you very much.* **George Farrant**'s *arrival breaks the conversation. He is about his wife's age; a pleasant, very honest fellow, bred to big affairs, but with no other particular qualification for them. Yet this, allied to his honesty and good nature, has let him hold his place among them respectably enough.*

Farrant Blackborough's going, Julia.

Lady Julia I thought he must have gone. What time is it?

Farrant Ten past eleven.

Lady Julia   Well . . . you've had something of a talk, you four.

Amy O'Connell   What about . . . or can't we be told?

Farrant   About the Goths in Italy and the Normans in Sicily . . . Maltese fever . . . Marriage in Morocco . . . Witchcraft . . . Oliver Cromwell and the Jews . . . William III's love affairs and Bergson's philosophy. I forget what else.

Russell Blackborough *follows his host into the room. One might more suitably say that he arrives. For to arrive is his vocation, and he by no means agrees with the proverb-maker that to travel is better. He is an able man; he has all the virtues that make for success, and, if sensitiveness is not among them, yet he is not an unkindly man. His voice, perhaps, is louder than it need be; and even when he is silent you always know he is there.*

Blackborough   Good-bye, Lady Julia. A delightful weekend.

Lady Julia   Whatever hour will you be home?

Blackborough   Not before the moon's down. But I'm due in Birmingham bright and early tomorrow. Good-bye, Lady Mortimer.

He is rounding the room with his good-byes.

Lady Mortimer   You're a marvel, Mr Blackborough. And never a holiday, you were telling me.

Blackborough   I hate holidays. Want to know my secret?

Amy O'Connell   Oh . . . please!

Blackborough   Learn to sleep at odd moments.

Amy O'Connell   In public?

Blackborough   Yes.

Amy O'Connell   That's no advice to give a woman.

Blackborough   Why not?

Amy O'Connell   I saw you asleep after tea. Good-bye.

The pin-point does not prick him. Thick-skinned he may be, but, to do him justice, he has no unmanly vanities.

Blackborough   Besides . . . we poor politicians must work double shifts for our bread and butter while we're in opposition. It's hardly safe when you're in office to hold on to a share . . . much less a directorship. How's the wretched capitalist to live? We can't all have copper magnates for great-grandfathers like you, Farrant . . . or be company lawyers like your brother . . . and they'd not have him in public life in America, Miss Trebell. Sorry I missed the music.

He really is. He likes music and the vigour of it. He sang in the Leeds choir in his young days.

Lady Julia   I left you alone. I thought you'd be talking shop.

Blackborough   No, no, no . . . we'd no shop to talk. And when will Horsham talk shop if he can help it? Idealist philosophy we finished with. That counts me out . . . I don't know the jargon. But I strongly suspect there's not too much sense in anything that can't be discussed in language the ordinary educated man can understand.

*The **Butler** has entered.*

Butler   Mr Blackborough's car, My Lady.

Blackborough *has finished his round, but for **Walter Kent**. Standing by him, he addresses **Lady Julia**.*

Blackborough   Do you go campaigning? No . . . Farrant's seat is safe. Come and speak for me.

Lady Julia *(as who should say, with all courtesy: 'The impudence!')* I have never spoken in public in my life . . . and I never shall.

Blackborough *almost welcomes the snub;* **Lady Julia** *can impress him, though it would not become him to own it.*

Blackborough   Ah . . . that's the true Tory tradition. We've to leave it to you ladies, though, to keep it up nowadays.

Farrant   A September dissolution, too! Labour w o u l d let us in for that.

Lady Mortimer   Is it to please the partridges? But they have no votes yet, have they?

Amy O'Connell   Poor partridges . . . with nobody but nobodies left to shoot at them!

Farrant   I mean to get a fortnight, though . . . whatever happens.

Blackborough   We shall come back this time, I don't doubt. (*Then with masterful suddenness to* **Walter**.) Are we to find you a seat, young man?

Walter Kent   Not yet, thank you. I've my trade to learn.

Blackborough   Trebell's taking you on.

Walter Kent   Yes.

Blackborough (*though somehow he doesn't seem to mean quite – quite – what he says*)   Lucky fellow! You'll learn a lot.

Farrant   Classical tripos at Cambridge. Now he has to go to Pitman's for shorthand and typewriting.

Blackborough   A year at the Central Office would have done you some good. I could have got you in there. Our young men in the House don't start by learning . . . as they ought . . . how a party is run and how votes are got.

Walter Kent (*very simply: one likes him for it*)   I think I'm more interested in ideas.

Blackborough   Then why go in for politics?

Lady Julia   Really, Mr Blackborough!

Blackborough (*genially*)   I know, I know . . . that raises a laugh from the intellectual snobs. Ideas have their place, undoubtedly. We need them to draw upon. But the statesman's task is the accommodation of stubborn fact to shifting circumstance . . . and in effect to the practical capacities of the average stupid man. Democracy involves the admission of that.

Lady Julia (*whose patience is being tried*)   I am at least not a democrat, Mr Blackborough.

Blackborough   Nor I . . . more of a democrat than I need to be. We've all to bow down a bit nowadays in the House of Rimmon. But, stampede people with ideas . . . ! Why . . . look at the Russian Revolution . . . look at the Chinese Revolution . . . look at India . . . look at Poplar. We live in dangerous times.

Lady Mortimer   So my dear grandfather used to say.

Blackborough   And no doubt he was right. The salvation of this country so far has been its imperviousness to abstract ideas. The difficulty of doing anything definite by party politics . . . strange as this sounds . . . is what keeps us sane and lets us get on with our business. I am a good enough democrat to wish to save democracy from itself . . . and from the ideologue and the doctrinaire. And I wish very much that this present government weren't leaving us such a crop of problems to deal with. The Dominion Treaties . . . the Emigration muddle . . . Disestablishment! They're shown great political wisdom in leaving us to tackle them. Well . . . we must just keep our heads and go slow . . . go slow. Good-night . . . good-night.

These last farewells have the savour of businesslike blessings. He departs and **Farrant** *hardly allows himself a smile as he follows him to see him off. But the rest of the company is visibly relieved.*

Lady Mortimer   Most impressive.

Amy O'Connell   Shouldn't we have cheered, or said 'Order' or 'Divide' or something?

Frances Trebell   Alas . . . one must never suppose a man a fool because he t a l k s nonsense.

Lady Julia   And I begged George to see he had his say after dinner. He'd been saving that up for t h e m . . . and he empties it all over u s. I will not be called an intellectual snob by Mr Blackborough. Is he out of my house yet?

Walter Kent   I expect so.

Lady Julia   Then I consider him a hog of a man.

Having said so, she forgives **Mr Blackborough**.

Lady Mortimer   But why have you let the Blackboroughs of this world become a power in your party, Julia?

Lady Julia   They think they are.

Lady Mortimer   I should give this one a peerage without more delay.

Lady Julia   Heavens . . . he wouldn't take it. I know . . . we used to quiet them that way. He wants the Treasury . . . and he'll get it some day, I suppose. He's useful . . . he knows where the votes come from . . . and he does raise funds from people that one really couldn't truckle to oneself. And if it pleases him to imagine that he 'bosses' us . . .

Lady Mortimer   Julia, don't be complacent. The man rattles you in his pocket with the rest of his loose change.

Lady Julia   Well, Mamma . . . if you'll tell me how to prevent undesirable people joining a party . . . we'll all be very much obliged to you.

Farrant *has returned, and finds himself opposite* **Mrs O'Connell**.

Farrant   How's the headache?

Amy O'Connell   Oh, I had a headache? So I had. No one pitied me. That must have cured it.

Farrant   Come on and play one game of pool. Good exercise. Come along, you two.

This last is to **Lucy** *and* **Walter**. **Lady Julia***'s eyebrows go up.*

Lady Julia   Dear George . . . at this hour!

Lucy Davenport   I'll play.

Lady Julia   Send Mr Trebell in to us. He won't, I'm sure.

Farrant   He said he'd a brief to look through. Shocking Sabbath-breaking!

Amy O'Connell   What a wonderful moon!

The suggestion of pool has shifted **Mrs O'Connell**.

Lady Julia   Dear George . . . at this he parted . . . ?

Farrant   Who's that? Oh, Blackborough.

Lady Julia   Did they get on any sort of terms, d'you think?

Farrant   I daresay. There's often more gained by not talking about a thing than just by talking.

Lady Julia   We really ought to have got one step further.

Farrant   Don't scold me . . . I did my devil-most. Why didn't you ask His Eminence Charles Cantilupe down? Then we'd have had Disestablishment hot for breakfast and cold for lunch . . . and Disestablishment nicely warmed up again for dinner.

Lady Julia   Yes . . . just what we didn't want at this juncture.

Farrant   Oh! Sorry I'm not subtle. (*Grumbling contentedly.*) I'm sick of politics. Nothing but a safe seat and a devotion to my country . . .

Lucy Davenport   Why don't you take a peerage, Cousin George?

Farrant   I'd love it. Julia won't let me.

Frances Trebell   Oh . . . why not?

Farrant   Julia, the daughter of a hundred earls . . . Julia, the wife of a pinchbeck modern peer! No, no! She married me for my money . . . and I must keep in my place.

Lady Julia   George . . . your humour is old-fashioned. Run away.

The two of them must be very happy together if he can joke with the truth like that. He turns towards the window. **Mrs O'Connell** *is standing right out in the moonlight now, but when he speaks to her she frames herself in the window again to answer him.*

Farrant   Come and take a cue, dear lady.

Amy O'Connell   Kind gentleman . . . did you never remark that I have a pointed elbow?

Farrant (*who is perhaps not quite so simple as he seems*)   No . . . have you?

Amy O'Connell   If I took a cue, you would. My headache's back . . . and the moon's very good for it. I shall stroll once round the fountain. And so to bed, Julia?

Lady Julia   Yes . . . biscuits are by the billiard-room. We'll pick you up there.

Amy O'Connell   I may be rude and not wait for you.

She vanishes into the moonlight and the garden. **Farrant** *departs.* **Lucy** *and* **Walter** *are about to follow him.*

Lady Julia   Oh dear, oh dear! I'm growing old . . . I'm growing clumsy. Here's the weekend over . . . and nothing has happened. And I thought I'd made up the mixture so nicely too. Lucy! Take Amy O'Connell her lace . . . or she'll catch a cold next.

Lucy *returns and picks up the lace scarf as if, it would seem, she had a certain contempt for it.*

Lucy Davenport   Colds are unbecoming.

Lady Julia   Lucy!

Lucy Davenport   Sorry! My claws need cutting. Here, Walter . . . you take it. Be gallant. You're forgetting how . . . hob-nobbing with me.

Walter Kent   That's your fault.

There is a happy, straightforward confidence in his voice which can have nothing to do, surely, with what he says. He goes after **Mrs O'Connell** *and* **Lucy** *after her cousin* **George**. *The three women left together settle at once into cosier friendliness.*

Lady Mortimer   Are those two young people engaged or are they not, Julia?

Lady Julia   No . . . but they settled when they were children that neither of them would ever marry anybody else. They haven't twopence. He thinks he ought to go into the City for a few years. She won't have that . . . he's to start for a career straight away. She's to have babies . . . two boys and a girl, she tells me.

Lady Mortimer   Science is so accommodating nowadays.

Lady Julia   She has the brains really . . . but he wants to please her. He'll be somebody before she has done.

Lady Mortimer   It was good of your Henry to give him such a chance.

Frances Trebell   My Henry wanted to please. And likes Walter. He doesn't like many people.

Lady Julia   Your Henry has been very naughty this weekend.

Frances Trebell   Julia, I did warn you . . . you may be wasting your time.

Lady Mortimer   Julia . . . if a brutal question is permissible: What are you up to?

Lady Julia   I hoped it was obvious. The successful intriguer, Mamma, does nothing underhand. If Cyril Horsham forms a Cabinet, Mr Trebell must be in it.

Lady Mortimer   But he doesn't belong to your party.

Lady Julia   He doesn't belong to any other. He sits as an Independent . . . Ellesmere's his pocket-borough. He always has got in as an Independent, hasn't he, Frances?

Frances Trebell   During the war –

Lady Julia   Oh, that doesn't count. And I want him to have charge of the Disestablishment Bill.

Lady Mortimer   That'll be a bold stroke.

Lady Julia   It's high time we made one . . . if we're not to be Blackboroughed to death.

Lady Mortimer   But won't it be Cyril's own affair?

Lady Julia   He can't . . . he must take the Foreign Office.
Do you mean to tell me, Frances, that if Henry's made the
offer point-blank he'll say no?

Frances Trebell   I think it quite likely.

Lady Julia   But what is he in public life for at all then? He
can't stay in the House and make speeches that count . . .
count for votes! . . . and always refuse office. It's not right. He
needn't join the party even. Disestablishment is an exceptional
thing . . . there'll be a lot of cross-voting.

Lady Mortimer   But sanctified by office, he might stay in
it, you think?

Lady Julia (*countering her mother with perfect frankness*)   Yes . . .
I hope. Practical politics are party politics. And we'd be the
better off for him. Can't you use your influence, Frances?

Frances Trebell   Julia . . . though such a thing must seem
to you against nature . . . I have no influence with Henry . . .
and never have had, from the days when we played in our
suburban nursery together.

Lady Julia   But what does he want of life? He doesn't like
society . . .

Frances Trebell   No.

Lady Julia   He dislikes women, apparently.

Frances Trebell   He's pretty indifferent to them.

Lady Julia   He can't suspect me of wanting to flirt with him,
I hope. But whenever I try and talk to him the temperature
drops.

Lady Mortimer   He flattered an old lady at tea-time
yesterday with some very pleasant attentions.

Lady Julia   He considers you safe, Mamma.

Lady Mortimer   Then he has no right to. Mine is the
perfect age for a love affair.

Lady Julia   How old is he, Frances?

Frances Trebell   Fifty-one.

Lady Julia   Well . . . he has made himself a unique position. If it's going to be a barren one . . . what a pity! And here's a chance of the premiership for him . . . nothing less in the end. Isn't that good enough? If you can't do better with him, Frances . . . marry him off to some vulgar ambitious woman who will.

Frances Trebell   I think I have never really known what Henry believed in. We all disbelieve in so much . . . and believe in so little nowadays.

The **Butler** *comes in.*

Butler   Dr Wedgecroft has telephoned, My Lady. His thanks . . . they stopped the express for him and he reached town in good time.

Lady Julia   Thank you.

The **Butler** *goes.*

Lady Mortimer   Was he sent for?

Lady Julia   No . . . it's his point of honour not to sleep out of town during what he calls his duty months.

Frances Trebell   Gilbert can do as much with Henry as anyone.

Lady Julia   I know. That's why I fetched him down today. They had a talk before dinner. Bed, Mamma?

Lady Mortimer   I think so.

Lady Julia   I must go by the billiard-room. Is our lovely Amy still star-gazing? Mr Blackborough didn't seem to be so very 'took' with her.

Lady Mortimer   He eyed her as if he thought she'd try to borrow money from him.

Frances Trebell   I don't see her.

The suggestion of bed has brought them to their feet; **Lady Mortimer** *is collecting her spectacles and suchlike;* **Frances** *has moved out to the courtyard; she now comes back.*

Lady Julia   I only asked her in the hope that she'd amuse him.

Frances Trebell   Julia . . . how brutal!

Lady Julia   People must expect to be made use of. She sets out to be amusing . . . to men. A house-party needs just a dash of . . . her sort of thing.

Lady Mortimer   Your cunning is too consistent, Julia. You really should do something single-minded occasionally. Why, by the way, did you ask me?

Lady Julia   I love you, Mamma.

Lady Mortimer   That may be your salvation yet.

Lady Julia   But the lovely Amy bores me. I wonder you like her so, Frances.

Frances Trebell   I like all sorts of people.

Lady Julia   Why doesn't she go back to her Justin?

Frances Trebell   He's impossible.

Lady Julia   I doubt it.

Frances Trebell   My dear . . . with a housemaid for his mistress . . . even an Irish housemaid!

Lady Julia   She could give her a month's notice.

Lady Mortimer   And this is the result of bringing up my daughter upon the novels of Miss Charlotte M. Yonge!

Frances Trebell   But for all Amy's airs and graces one feels sorry for her at times. There's something of the waif about her.

Lady Mortimer   Good-night, dear Miss Trebell.

Frances Trebell   Good-night.

Lady Julia   I'll come in and kiss you, Mamma. And I will not sit up watching Lucy play pool . . .

And so they talk themselves out of the room.

It must be an hour later, or nearly, for the moon has sunk behind the little wooded hills which bound the gardens. The room is empty. Some thrifty hand has turned out a light or two. In the courtyard there appear **Amy O'Connell** *and* **Henry Trebell.** *The lace scarf that* **Walter** *took her is wrapped around her head and shoulders: she looks nun-like. They pause outside the window.*

Amy O'Connell   There goes the moon . . . so there goes romance! I'm cold. Doesn't moonshine warm the night just a little?

Trebell   No.

Amy O'Connell   Sure?

Trebell   Quite.

Amy O'Connell   I like to think it does.

She comes into the room; he follows her. We are all built upon contradictions; hence our equilibrium. But with most of us the opposing qualities are fused in compromise. What one remarks in **Trebell** *is that with him this is not so. The idealist and the cynic, the sensualist and the ascetic, gentleness and cruelty, could any one of them have undisputed sway if he'd let them. But not the least remarkable thing about him is the rigid control which some inner man seems to exercise over this outer man, yet with indifference, almost with disdain. At this moment, however, he is flirting with a pretty woman. He flirts a little grimly. There is something, one would say, cat-like about* **Mrs O'Connell**, *and one might compare her flirting – the metaphor is none the worse for being old – to the cat playing with its mouse. But a tiger is playing with her.*

Amy O'Connell   Everyone in bed?

Trebell   The billiard-room lights are out.

Amy O'Connell   How rude of Julia! What's the time?

Trebell   Twenty past twelve.

Amy O'Connell (*happily horror-struck*)   Never! Then how dare you keep me gallivanting in the garden all this while? No one told you I was down there?

Trebell   No.

Amy O'Connell   That's as well.

Trebell   They thought you'd carried your headache to bed . . .

Amy O'Connell   I hope.

Trebell   I went off to finish some work. I slipped out for a breath of fresh air . . . and took a bee-line to you.

Amy O'Connell   In the dark!

Trebell   By instinct.

Amy O'Connell   Well, good-night.

Trebell   Good-night.

She gives him her hand, which he holds a moment longer than he need.

Amy O'Connell   But you've been dodging me this whole weekend . . . publicly.

Trebell   I have been dodging you . . . privately . . . for these last six months.

Amy O'Connell   Then . . . let me tell you . . . you began to dodge long before there was any need.

Trebell   I felt the need.

Amy O'Connell   Thank you. I'm such a siren, am I . . . *malgré moi?* I'll see there's no more need. How long since we first met?

Trebell   I fear I forget.

Amy O'Connell   It's a year or more. I disliked you then exceedingly.

Trebell   I make no complaint of that.

Amy O'Connell   Last January I began to like you a little . .
. and for one whole evening I thought you liked me. After that
I disliked you till about April . . . then for a week or two I liked
you a lot. But I think I'd better finish by disliking you.

Trebell   Perhaps you had.

Amy O'Connell   Have you any friends?

Trebell   Only old friends.

Amy O'Connell   You'll chaff and flatter and gibe at me
for an hour. But you don't like me . . . so why not say so?
Good-night.

*She is close to him. Without preliminaries he seizes her and kisses her,
full on the lips. Having done so he releases her as suddenly. She stands
there, a challenger, whose challenge has been accepted. But there is to be
manoeuvring yet.*

Amy O'Connell   And you'll do that! I might have known.

Trebell   Didn't you?

Amy O'Connell   One has to risk it.

Trebell   I've not kissed a woman for ten years . . . just about.

Amy O'Connell (*pursing her numbed lips prettily*)   So I should
suppose!

Trebell   I apologise. No I don't. You knew that I'd kiss you.

Amy O'Connell   Really! Which is the worse? The kiss . . .
or the apology . . . or that? I wonder if I could be as brutal as
you, Henry. Shall I try?

Trebell   Do try.

Amy O'Connell   If you meant to . . . why didn't you . . .
before? It was wonderful there by the fountain. I'll confess,
when we turned down by the yew trees . . . I did think you
would.

Trebell No! I've no taste for romance in the moonlight. Nor any time . . . nor taste for semi-intellectual flirtations. You're quite right . . . you'd better keep away from me.

Amy O'Connell What has made you so afraid of women? Did some selfish creature try to marry you? I wonder any man gets married. Why should he? But I rather wonder you weren't married young . . . and married wrong. Almost any woman could have married you . . . if she'd put her mind to it.

Trebell I was engaged for a year or more when I was twenty-two. For I was a nice young man . . .

Amy O'Connell Never!

Trebell By bringing up . . . by habit . . . heading for domesticity. Yes . . . and it was by moonlight in a garden I proposed.

Amy O'Connell Such an indelicate word, I always think! Did she jilt you, the silly? Did you suffer?

Trebell No . . . I broke it off . . . I had the pluck to.

Amy O'Connell Why?

Trebell I never can want to see things but just starkly as they are. She was a nice young woman through and through . . . and full of sentiments that she thought were feelings and of shop-soiled ideas. Incurably suburban and incurably unreal. And she wasn't for babies and housekeeping. We were to be life-long companions in culture. I should have broken her heart. She never married. Frances keeps in touch with her. She settled in Surrey . . . has a garden . . . and belongs to the Labour Party. Later . . . if this interests you . . .

Amy O'Connell But of course it interests me.

Trebell It ought not to . . . at the moment.

Amy O'Connell Why not?

Trebell The past has no place in love-making . . . nor the future.

Amy O'Connell   Oh . . . are we love-making?

Trebell   I'm waiting to begin again.

Amy O'Connell   Then I'd better hear about your past . . . while there's still time.

Trebell   It's not interesting. I had an affair . . . as they're called . . . with a woman, which worked out like the plot of a cheap novel. Really we might have been reading it up as we went . . . she and her husband and I. It must have been about their sixth volume. He'd been the first one's hero. Then he had to encourage successors . . . or the useless, unhappy creature would have taken to drink or religion or something. I escaped. Good honest harlotry is more tolerable than that. No . . . thank you very much . . . no more hectic half-hours or moonlit moments for me.

Amy O'Connell   But has no woman ever made you suffer? Not that you'd tell me!

Trebell   I daresay I shouldn't.

Amy O'Connell   Never a heartache.

Trebell   When you talk of stomach-ache I know what you mean. When you talk of heartache . . . I'm not so sure y o u do!

Amy O'Connell   I do not talk of stomach-aches . . . and I never have one.

Trebell   Lucky woman!

Amy O'Connell   There's no luck in it . . . I'm particular about my food. But I wonder if I couldn't make you suffer . . . just a little.

Trebell   I doubt it.

Amy O'Connell   You'd come to thank me. All that is best in my character I owe to unhappiness.

Trebell   This is where I kiss you again.

Amy O'Connell   Thank you for the warning. It's where you don't.

Trebell Silly talk of some sort seems a necessary prelude . . . though I never could make out why. I've obliged with my share . . . I hoped we were through with it. But do let us avoid cant!

Amy O'Connell Henry . . . you're right . . . I'd better have done with you. You're a cold-blooded brute.

Trebell Far from it.

Amy O'Connell Well . . . you've given what you'd call your heart, then, to politics and the law. I daresay you're quite sentimental about tariffs and the gold standard. But wherever should I come in? Join the Tories and let Julia patronise you. You'll find that frightfully thrilling. I wish I'd never begun to like you. Heavens . . . you must be horrid to live with! Poor Frances!

Trebell She has not been complaining, I hope.

Amy O'Connell Not she! I love Frances.

Trebell I constantly hear you say so.

Amy O'Connell And she adores you.

Trebell With the subtlety of vanity I divined what you and she had in common.

Amy O'Connell I wish you thought you were vain. There'd be that much more humanity about you.

Trebell The very first time I saw you . . . you were sitting on the sofa by the fireplace in Berkeley Street . . . Frances was giving you tea . . . there were three of four other women there. You wore a pink dress with frills to it.

Amy O'Connell Lilac! Heavens . . . I never wore pink in my life!

Trebell It was pink to me! And when you arched your instep . . . it's a trick you have . . . I could hear the stocking rustle.

Amy O'Connell   I'd forgotten you were there. I'm so glad I'd forgotten.

Trebell   If I'd followed my instinct then I should have sat down and made love to you before them all . . . which wouldn't quite have done.

Amy O'Connell   And since then you've had so much else to do!

Trebell   My day's work's pretty dull. I've grown so used to doing it.

Amy O'Connell   Such brilliant speeches to make!

Trebell   I've grown used to making 'em. No . . . I rather regretted then that the temptation of you wasn't overwhelming. But we have our wintry seasons . . . long ones, often!

Amy O'Connell   I don't want to tempt you. Yes, I do. But you don't look one bit . . . even now . . . as if you were in love with me. Yes, you do . . . yes, you do. But you've not said you love me. Why don't you say so?

Trebell   I'll say whatever's necessary.

Amy O'Connell   Don't gibe! I hate you when you gibe. Not even asked me if I love you!

Trebell   Don't you? Do you? Don't you?

Amy O'Connell   We don't mean the same thing by it, I'm afraid.

Trebell   It comes to the same thing.

Amy O'Connell   Henry . . . you have a coarse mind! No . . . I'll have nothing to do with you.

Trebell   Very well.

Amy O'Connell   I won't be played with. Oh . . . it has always been the same. I was petted and bullied as a child . . . one or the other or both at a time. Justin petted and spoiled and bullied me till he got sick of it . . . and I got sick of it and left him. I was very unhappy with Justin. Well . . . I made him unhappy, I suppose.

Trebell   Still, he was able in the interval to write two books that count on Plantagenet charters.

Amy O'Connell   Do they? I'm sure I'm very glad. I suppose it would be kinder now to divorce him. But I can't make up my mind to . . . for we're Catholics . . . and I haven't any money of my own. And whatever I did he'd never divorce me.

Trebell   Well . . . that gives you scope.

Amy O'Connell   Oh no, no . . . you don't take me seriously! I'm good for something more than to be treated like this. And I will be!

They have been sitting together on the sofa, close together. But all this time he has not even touched her hand. Now, though, he takes her in his arms and begins to kiss her, not once but again and again, not hastily either.

Trebell   This is how I take you . . . seriously . . . very seriously. Isn't this serious enough?

She gasps, half ecstatic, or a little frightened.

Amy O'Connell   Let me get my breath.

Trebell   No, I won't.

He holds her still, and still kisses her.

Isn't this good enough . . . almost?

He half releases her at last. If he quite let her go she would fall.

Say something.

Amy O'Connell (*softly*)   I've nothing to say.

Trebell   Kiss me.

She is lifting her lips obediently when she hears footsteps.

Amy O'Connell   Good Heavens . . . somebody's coming.

Trebell   One of the servants. Sit still.

Amy O'Connell No, no . . . he'll notice . . . ! Oh, what a fool . . . to be caught . . . !

She has vanished through the window. **Trebell** *is sitting at his ease as the* **Butler** *comes in, evidently to close the room. This promises a dilemma. As* **Trebell** *does not move, after a moment the* **Butler** *asks discreetly . . .*

Butler You're sitting up, sir?

Trebell No . . . I've just been for a walk . . . round the ponds . . . I didn't know it was so late. The house looks its best by moonlight.

Butler Yes, sir . . . the Inigo Jones wing especially . . . so it's considered.

Trebell It is Inigo Jones?

Butler Most houses that can like to call themselves that . . . but there's his accounts for the work in the library. I have the drawing-rooms to see closed yet, sir.

He is on his way out by the other door.

Trebell Oh . . . what about trains in the morning?

Butler There's the 8.45 . . . the 9.30's a slow . . . and a 10.14.

Trebell What time in town?

Butler Ten past eleven.

Trebell I must take the early one. I don't want breakfast. A cup of coffee.

Butler Very good, sir.

The **Butler** *departs.* **Trebell***, after two seconds' assurance that he has departed, goes up to the window.*

Trebell All clear!

Amy *slips back through the window, and is making a bee-line for the door when he catches her hand. She is tremulous, but too stirred to be frightened. She tugs, though.*

Amy O'Connell　Good-night . . . good-night!

Trebell　No.

Amy O'Connell　My darling . . . good-night.

Trebell　Not at all.

Amy O'Connell　Henry . . . let me go.

Trebell　Your room's the last on the left?

She gasps.

Amy O'Connell　Oh no! No . . . it isn't.

Trebell　Never mind . . . there are cards on the doors . . . most sensible custom!

Amy O'Connell　No, no . . . oh, for Heaven's sake, no! Not here!

Trebell　Why ever not!

Amy O'Connell　Not tonight, though . . . Henry . . . please!

Trebell　We may both be dead by tomorrow. I'll wait half an hour.

Amy O'Connell　Don't make me ashamed. Let's be patient a little. That'll make it more beautiful. I promise . . . I promise you . . . very soon.

Trebell　I can't stop you turning your key.

Amy O'Connell　Then you'll say I'm being heartless. Is he coming back?

Trebell　Yes.

*The advent of the **Butler** whips her share of the dispute to a small frenzy. He holds her still, but if she struggled a little harder, surely she could break away. It is not his hand's grip that holds her, distracted, possessed, pathetic.*

Amy O'Connell　. . . and I'm not. No, nor patient . . . in my heart. I love you . . . it hurts me to love you so. Yours . . .

all of me . . . whenever . . . whenever . . . ! Oh, I can't stop
here arguing!

*With which sudden break into the commonplace and almost with a stamp
of the foot she breaks free and vanishes. He is finding a book to take up to
bed with him when the* **Butler** *returns one moment later.*

Trebell   Good-night.

Butler   Good-night, sir.

Trebell *goes off with his book. The* **Butler** *starts to close the room.*

Act Two

Trebell *has just moved into a fresh working room in his house in Berkeley Street, though* **Frances**, *to be sure, did the moving. The room shows new, but not aggressively. It shows also in its white paint, its plain beige walls, its barely curtained windows, its spareness of ornament, his taste (and hers) for simplicity in such matters, above all, for plentiful light by which to work. You can read a book in any corner of it.*

The two long windows on your left throw their light well across the room. Facing you is a double door; when this is opened another door is seen across the landing (we are on the first floor); and when this is opened you can see a writing-table with its furnishings. And the walls for this smaller room, which is, so to speak, an under-study, are lined with bookcases filled with law reports and suchlike. Between the two rooms a window throws light on the landing and up and down the staircase. In **Trebell**'s *room the bookcases are low, they run all around it, and the books are of every sort and kind. On one side of the bright fire, which is on your right, there is an armchair. On the other a chaise-longue sticks out, and by each are tables piled with books. There is yet another table with newspapers ranged on it in order. And, standing out in the room, is a very large writing-table, covered – besides its proper belongings, its big ink-stand, its telephone – with books, blue-books, pamphlets and a hundred letters or so, opened and unopened, neatly placed in packets, elastic-banded. And at the table sits* **Trebell** *himself, surveying the work he has evidently just come back to, and beginning to nibble at it.* **Frances** *looks in on him. She is dressed to go out; by the look of her dress it is a fine autumn morning.*

Frances Trebell   Henry . . . I'm off now. I've ordered lunch for you. There's enough for two if you want to feed Walter.

Trebell   I've given him this morning to spend with his beloved. But I do wish that nice young man hadn't settled to marry just as this job was starting. And he didn't tell me until the ship was half way to Naples . . . or I'd never have taken him on the jaunt.

Frances Trebell   Lucy made him go.

Trebell   I wish they were married, then, and had got their romancing over.

Frances Trebell   You're their romance.

Trebell   Heaven help me!

Frances Trebell   And your job. It's a big job.

Trebell   It has the makings of a job in it.

Frances Trebell   Is this room all right? The paint still smells a bit. I had to put *Hansard* and the big dictionaries and most of the books from the Temple in there.

Trebell   I admire my wastepaper basket (*which is, indeed, magnificently capacious*).

Frances Trebell   The statesman's companion. Everything has been answered that could be. There are the press-cuttings. You do look the sounder for six weeks in Italy.

Trebell   That stretch east of Rome that nobody ever sees is worth seeing. I escaped the election babel anyhow. Thank Heaven I didn't have to fight.

Frances Trebell   It was a near thing, though, they didn't run that Labour man against you.

Trebell   But when the car broke something . . . which it did most days . . . Kent and I would climb up out of the dust and sit making up fifteenth-century campaigning speeches to the citizens of Cassino or Lanciano or Bovino or wherever it was we ought to have been getting to while Giacomo Giuseppe Giusti tied it up again with bits of string.

Frances Trebell   It rained hard here all September. This month has been beautiful so far.

Trebell   How long did you stay at Winfield?

Frances Trebell   Till Mary was up again.

Trebell   A boy or a girl? You did tell me.

Frances Trebell   Another girl.

Trebell   A dull holiday for you.

Frances Trebell   No . . . I'm not sure I wasn't meant to live
in a Dorset rectory.

Trebell   Sorry I took the wrong turning. The thing to
remember about the Renaissance Italian is that he was a
realist . . . a financier . . . a passionate politician . . . who took
beauty and art and literature and the rest in his stride. An
immoral fellow . . . Hullo!

This last is to **Walter Kent** *who has just bounded up the stairs,
glanced into the little room, which is his own, and now turns into this.
He is in fine trim, and happy beyond words: not so much at being on the
threshold of his own career as in his share of his hero's.*

Walter Kent   I got Lord Charles on the telephone. He'd
rather come and see you. He said eleven-thirty.

Trebell   That'll do.

Walter Kent   I'd better begin on these.

He takes a packet or so of the already opened letters from the table.

Trebell   What about Wedgecroft?

Walter Kent   He's here.

Trebell   I gave you the morning off, you know.

Walter Kent   I know.

Walter *carries his letters into his room.* **Frances** *stands watching him,
affectionately amused; time was when she dashed at work like that. He
does not deliberately ignore her, of course; they have evidently met before
this morning. A* **Maid** *now announces 'Dr Wedgecroft', whom* **Frances**
turns to greet. **Wedgecroft** *is a man of* **Trebell***'s age, if to outward
appearance rather older, but alert in body and mind; a born healer, his
bedside manner real and not assumed; one discerns an intellectual
ruthlessness in him too.*

Wedgecroft   How are you?

Frances Trebell   You need never ask.

Wedgecroft   You wait! Once I start physicking you . . . !
Have you come back ill?

He has passed on to **Trebell**. *Not having met for months, they are yet too close friends for any hand-shaking.*

Trebell   No.

Wedgecroft   Then how dare you drag me from Wimpole Street?

Trebell   I've a better use for you. Give me five minutes.

Frances *is departing.* **Walter** *comes to the door of his room.* **Wedgecroft** *goes up for a word with him.* **Trebell** *has not moved from his table.*

Frances Trebell   In to dinner, Henry?

Trebell   Yes . . . no . . . I don't know.

Frances Trebell   I'll ask Julia . . . if she's doing nothing . . . and your young lady (*this to* **Walter**). You'll be here . . . let me tell you . . . till midnight.

Wedgecroft   How long do I have to decide between a set of fish-knives and a sugar-sifter?

Walter Kent   I should start to think about it.

Frances Trebell   Oh . . . and Walter, if Amy O'Connell rings up . . . No . . . never mind. I'll leave a message downstairs. She asked us to Charles Street . . . vaguely. Whatever time she wakes in the morning . . . !

Frances *is already half-way downstairs.* **Walter** *goes back into his room.* **Wedgecroft** *returns to* **Trebell**, *and the two are at ease for their talk.* **Trebell** *looks at the other a little quizzically as if he expected* **Wedgecroft** *to have something to say to him – and he has.*

Trebell   Well?

Wedgecroft   Henry . . . I consider you owe me an apology.

Trebell   Do you?

Wedgecroft   When did you settle this?

Trebell   With Horsham . . . definitely? . . . though, of course, it can't be definite till he is sent for. Ten days before I left.

Wedgecroft   And just about three weeks before that I was walking you round the garden at Shapters . . . persuading you –

Trebell   The good Lady Julia having set you on.

Wedgecroft   And you quite persuaded me that you'd be wrong to.

Trebell   Did I? What excellent arguments did I use?

Wedgecroft   You said you were no Tory –

Trebell   Notoriously no Tory!

Wedgecroft   Psychologists declare the punning habit to be a sign of failing intellect.

Trebell   They're wrong. The passionate pun is a feature of great literature. But I'm not a Liberal, am I?

Wedgecroft   I have never accused you of altruism.

Trebell   I might join the Liberals . . . if I were twenty.

Wedgecroft   You said you'd made Labour loathe you by ten years' damning of the Trades Unions –

Trebell   And I've been right! Look at their candidates this last election. Good God . . . a feudal system working from the bottom up? Who wants that?

Wedgecroft   So you could be no help to Horsham there?

Trebell   Oh . . . the Labour front bench loves to hear me damning the Unions. They look down their noses like pleased pussy-cats. They daren't do it themselves.

Wedgecroft   What made you change your mind?

Trebell   That's my secret. Have you been seeing Horsham?

Wedgecroft   Once or twice. He's been at Lympne . . . pretty tired out.

Trebell   These present fellows mean to meet Parliament . . .

Wedgecroft   Apparently.

Trebell He'll have to beat 'em on the Address.

Wedgecroft You won't be in office until mid-November.

Trebell I'm not in all that hurry. It's a simple secret,
Gilbert. I found I'd fallen in love. No . . . not with a woman,
you old sentimentalist! With this job. I am in love with a Bill
for the Disestablishment of the Church of England . . . and for
doing sundry more interesting things. And I mean to make an
honest Act of Parliament of the little darling. I'm as joyful . . .
as that lad is in there at his prospect of answering my letters
for a year or two. But I don't show it.

Wedgecroft Don't you . . . my innocent?

Trebell Do I? Well, I don't care if I do.

Wedgecroft I'm glad . . . I'm damned glad. I'd begun to
wonder about you. I seem to have watched so many rivers run
into the sand.

Trebell Men get what they want in this world mostly. The
hard thing is to want it . . . and to keep on wanting it . . .
and to want nothing else. I thought the law altogether lovely
once . . . till I learned to make twelve thousand a year out of it.
I went into the House quite hopefully. But my only choice
there came to be between gibing at the fools and becoming
one of them.

Wedgecroft Now, now . . . are they all fools?

Trebell There are the worse-than-fools . . . that see the facts
and shirk them. Do our bodies ever come to disbelieve in life?

Wedgecroft Sometimes.

Trebell Then you've soon done with them?

Wedgecroft Not always.

Trebell Better to be. From barrenness of mind and emptiness
of will, at any rate, I'd pray . . . if I knew how to pray . . .
for death to deliver me. But we cling on . . . and sometimes
life delivers us. Most men's temptation, I suppose, is to make
for success . . . to learn the official creed of what we do n o t

believe . . . to attune themselves to the mob mind . . . till they
have earned their place among the parasites upon power that
call themselves governments today. It's not so hard a path . . .
to the dead end of success. But I wasn't tempted. I'm not built
that way.

Wedgecroft   And what's to be the difference now?

Trebell   You'll see. I hope you'll see.

Wedgecroft   Horsham's doing a plucky thing, Henry. What
will the real old Tories make of you?

Trebell   Oh, they'd kick . . . if they'd the spirit of their own
sheep.

Wedgecroft   And the rest of the crew? Blackborough?

Trebell   I'm not afraid of him.

Wedgecroft   He'll be at the Treasury?

Trebell   I hope not. He and his ca'canny business kind . . .
they've no right in government at all . . . they're as bad as the
Trades Unions every bit. Blackborough's a getter . . . not a
giver.

Wedgecroft   Cut out for the Treasury, then . . . he may
think. He doesn't love you.

Trebell   I daresay not.

Wedgecroft   There's a Cabinet sweepstake at the Club. I
drew Farrant.

Trebell   Oh . . . he'll be in. Nice fellow. No good, of course.
Agriculture, probably.

Wedgecroft   I sold him for a fiver.

Trebell   There'll have to be a fair lot of fresh men. Walter
and I sat in the Galleria at Milan last Thursday drinking
chocolate and trying to make a list. Yes . . . I can pull this Bill
through the House . . . I can face the public . . . I can stand up
to the press! But the thought of one's colleagues keeps one
awake at night. I want Cantilupe in.

Wedgecroft   Good Heavens . . . no!

Trebell   Why not?

Wedgecroft   My dear Henry! His Eminence . . . with every
incense-swinger in England at his back . . . in a Cabinet . . .
that's to disestablish the Church!

Trebell   He has come round to it.

Wedgecroft   Even so . . . will Broad Church and Low
Church and pretty-nearly-no-Church stomach his official
finger in the pie?

Trebell   They're to be bought. Endow their good works
department. The mammon of righteousness!

Wedgecroft   And the bishops?

Trebell   I can deal with the bishops. A bishop's a man of
business. He has to be . . . and it's all he has much chance to be.
But there's life in Cantilupe and his lot. They believe in
something bigger than the multiplication table. So do I . . .
though they don't give me credit for it. I can get something
out of them.

Wedgecroft   But, Henry . . . from your own standpoint . . .
when you've done this job . . . and it's going to be the devil of
a job . . . what's to happen then?

Trebell   What do you see happening then?

Wedgecroft   Why is it offered you?

Trebell *up to now has been shrewd, amused, reflective. This rouses in
him a certain dialectical pugnacity.*

Trebell   Because they've not a man among them that
doesn't funk it. Why must democracy grow us these crops of
political cowards? Two governments have shirked the thing . . .
Horsham would shirk it now if he could . . . though it has been
plain these ten years that something drastic must be done . . .
ever since the Jackson case . . . ever since the Anglo-Catholics
began to keep out non-communicants. And what has been

done? The Liberals meet at Manchester and cry: Down with
Dogma . . . Free Trade in Religion for ever . . . Take the
Endowments to pay off the War Debt . . . !

Wedgecroft   Now, now . . . be fair.

Trebell   Never be fair to your opponents . . . it wastes time.
All Labour can think of is: Pity the poor pew-opener . . .
double her old-age pension. I talk some sense on the subject.
So Horsham turns to me . . . and I may take any sort of a
settlement that will save him thinking of the thing again. And
then Blackborough and his back-scratching friends will pick a
quarrel with me . . . and out I may go into the wilderness with
whatever odium's in the Act when it's working on my back.

Wedgecroft   Well . . . as long as you foresee that part of the
programme too!

Trebell   That part mayn't come off, though.

Wedgecroft   Oh, they'll be glad enough to turn you Tory.
Dear Lady Julia will take you gently in hand . . . to add you to
the list of reformers she has reformed.

Trebell   I know! Damn all these women. Though she has
brains . . . of the ornamental sort. I don't think, though, she has
been good for Horsham. These spiritual adulteries debilitate
the mind. She'd better have been his mistress for a year or two
and have done with it.

Wedgecroft   But I do not see you leavening the Tory lump.

Trebell   Gilbert . . . when you fall in love don't look too
far ahead. Let your faith have its will of you. Here's a problem
in high politics . . . the first for how long that has not been
mere bread-and-butter business . . . set me to solve. I'm in love
with solving it. And my creed is belief in the thing done . . .
well and truly done as a means to the next. Not in the thing
shirked . . . in this fashionable fog of good-will . . . this power,
not ourselves, that makes for statesmanship. I believe if I dare
do this job ruthlessly . . . for its own sake . . . I can make the
thing done a living thing . . . a hopeful thing. And with a few
more such for a sign this dazed generation might pluck up

and face the future again. And I'll face a soft old age. But look here . . . this is what I want you for. How about Brampton?

Wedgecroft   I'm on my way round there.

Trebell   I thought you might be. How ill is he?

Wedgecroft   He's seventy-four.

Trebell   What's that nowadays? Is he really ill . . . is he going to die?

Wedgecroft   Sir . . . I am attending him.

Trebell   And why the devil do you let him get ill just now? Is he too ill to look through my figures? Horsham says he has had them three weeks.

At this moment the table telephone rings. **Trebell** *mechanically puts the receiver to his ear and holds it there while the talk goes on. But he receives nothing apparently.*

Wedgecroft   He has been ill enough to do nothing he didn't want to do.

Trebell (*to the telephone*)   Hullo? Yes? Hullo? Won't he stomach me as a colleague? Is that what's the matter with him?

Wedgecroft   Professional etiquette forbids me to disclose what a patient may confess in the sweat of his agony. But you may take it his stomach is sound.

Walter Kent *comes in and, seeing his chief clinging to the receiver, says, cheerfully* . . .

Walter Kent   Sorry . . . I wasn't sure if it worked.

Trebell   You and your new toy! Cantilupe?

Walter Kent   No. This from Mr Horsham. And Mrs O'Connell's downstairs. Miss Trebell's out. Are you both dining with her in Charles Street or not?

Trebell *opens the large envelope and goes through its contents as he talks.*

Trebell   I haven't the remotest idea. I shall work here till eight. Then I shall go where I'm taken . . . till ten.

Walter Kent   I could telephone to Lady Julia's . . . Miss Trebell may be there.

He goes back to his room to do so.

Wedgecroft   Does Horsham expect to bring the old man in?

Trebell   I want him at the Treasury.

Wedgecroft   In Blackborough's place?

Trebell   It isn't Blackborough's place.

Wedgecroft   You want all the troublesome fellows.

Trebell   I want all the first-rate fellows. These are my figures . . . sent back through Horsham. He has not made a note on them. What the devil's he up to?

Wedgecroft   I can tell you a bit of his mind. He knew I should see you . . . I fancy he meant me to. He detests this political generation. He thinks you're mad . . . but he rather admires you. He'll come back, he says, if he comes back at all, to knock your finance into shape, and some of the nonsense out of you. But for you, he thinks, Horsham's not got a man who won't muddle the job anyhow. So why the blankety blank blank . . . but for you . . . shouldn't he make ready to meet his God in peace?

Trebell   Good . . . !

*During this, **Mrs O'Connell** has come quietly up the stairs to stand, smiling and composed, on the landing. At this point they turn to see her.*

Amy O'Connell   Oh . . . this is y o u r room now? And I'm interrupting . . . I'm so sorry. Where's the drawing-room, then? And how are you? Had a good holiday? Not being physicked? How are y o u, dear Dr Wedgecroft? Do you and

Frances dine with me? Nothing's ordered now . . . so you can't. Why doesn't she answer my messages?

Still smiling, still composed – is she a little too composed? – she has come into the room for these greetings and questions. **Trebell** *is familiarly polite.*

Trebell Kent is telephoning to Frances. I'm very well, thank you. The new drawing-room is downstairs. I've had an excellent holiday. I think nothing of Gilbert as a doctor; but his political intelligence . . . in both senses . . . I prize.

Mrs O'Connell *is surveying the big writing-table now with mock-childish admiration.*

Amy O'Connell What a tableful! If I sit here, shall I know what it feels like to be a great man?

Wedgecroft How is Ireland?

Amy O'Connell Beautiful always, isn't it? But sad!

Wedgecroft I used to feel sad there. But that was my bad British conscience. I'm off, Henry.

Trebell *joins him at the door, and* **Mrs O'Connell** *is left sitting at the table. She takes up a pencil and a bit of paper and begins to scribble idly.*

Trebell The old man's my man . . . I don't mind what he thinks of me. He has forgotten more than I've ever learnt. He's got courage . . . he's got character. I'd sooner have him to fight than these political tradesmen to chaffer with. Get him out of bed . . . or give me half an hour with him and I'll get him out for you.

Walter Kent *has emerged from his room.*

Walter Kent I'm sorry . . . Miss Trebell's not there.

Amy O'Connell Thank you ever so much . . . it doesn't matter in the least.

Walter *goes back again.*

Wedgecroft   Well . . . when the thermometer's in his mouth
I'll say a word.

Trebell   Thank you for coming . . . and always thank you.

Now, as upon impulse, the two do shake hands; and then **Wedgecroft**,
half in fun, slips professional fingers to his friend's wrist.

Wedgecroft   I have backed you from the start. No, not for a
place . . . you could have had that any time, I knew . . . but to
win. Pulse . . . seventy. I'd prefer it a thought quicker.

Trebell   Why?

Wedgecroft   Good balance is good . . . but the power of
recovery is better . . . and Nature likes us to have a little
practice in it now and then. I've never yet seen you thrilled
or rattled.

Mrs O'Connell, *her scribbling over, has picked up from the table
between finger and thumb what looks like a large flint stone, used as a
paper weight evidently.*

Amy O'Connell   Whatever is this, Henry?

Trebell   I don't get rattled. I will at the next chance to please
you. That? . . . won me my first seat . . . flung at me out of the
first crowd I spoke to.

Amy O'Connell   Did your head make this chip in it?

Trebell   The fellow was a good shot. I wore a bandage for
a month. I owed him five hundred votes by polling day. But he
never let me thank him.

Wedgecroft *has gone. Beckoned by her voice,* **Trebell** *moves towards
her, and a tapping finger tells him to read over her shoulder what she has
scribbled on the scrap of paper. When he has read it he looks up to find*
Walter Kent *standing in the doorway as if waiting instructions.*

Walter Kent   No answer to Mr Horsham?

Trebell   No.

The word has perhaps an odd ring in it; but **Walter** *does not notice and goes downstairs to dismiss* **Horsham**'s *messenger.* **Trebell** *goes, not too quickly, to the door to shut it after him, while* **Amy O'Connell** *tears the scrap of paper into small bits, and throws them — a first sacrifice — into the so capacious wastepaper basket.*

Amy O'Connell   Don't shut the door. Yes . . . you'd better.

He does; then faces her. Her mask drops off.

Trebell   What's wrong?

Amy O'Connell   Why have you been away . . . these ages? I couldn't write. Come nearer to me. You'll hate me, Henry.

Trebell   Trouble with your husband?

Amy O'Connell   Not yet. No . . . I've not been near him. But you'd stopped loving me before you went away . . . after that one week. I knew. And you'll hate me now.

Her voice, too flat, too sharp, is hardly under her control. She is near the edge, indeed, of a nervous collapse.

Trebell   My dear girl . . . if you've anything to tell me that won't wait, tell it quickly. We shall be interrupted . . . at any moment.

She tells him . . .

Amy O'Connell   There's a danger of my having a child . . . your child . . . sometime in April. That's all.

Trebell   In April?

Amy O'Connell   The first week of April.

Trebell   You're sure?

Amy O'Connell   My God . . . d'you think I want it to be true? Say something.

He does not recognise, nor she, this echo of his own demand at a certain auspicious moment. But if he is silent, it is that his thoughts are racing.

Trebell   When did you last . . . see your husband?

Amy O'Connell   A year ago . . . and more.

Trebell   Yes. We must consider.

His tones are dry. Her voice is dead.

Amy O'Connell   I knew you'd hate me.

He is kindlier, but his mind is set neither to kindness nor unkindness.

Trebell   Nonsense, my dear! You've had a hard month or so . . . with no one to talk to. I'm sorry.

Amy O'Connell   I kept telling myself: it's not possible. Then . . . last Thursday week . . . I went to a doctor . . . down at Southampton . . . picked him out of the telephone book . . . gave him another name . . . told him I was off abroad. A kind old thing . . . said it was all quite satisfactory. But I've to keep telling myself it's true . . . or I shouldn't believe it. Though when I wake at night . . . each time I wake, I'm saying: Yes, of course it's true . . . you've known it all along. How can things happen so . . . in spite of one?

Trebell   Yes . . . you've not been sleeping . . . I can see.

Amy O'Connell   Kind of you to tell me . . . most consoling! No, I've not been. I've taken stuff . . . all I dare . . . all I could get. You can't get much.

Trebell   That won't do. You must be looked after.

Amy O'Connell   Who's one to trust? I nearly bolted when I saw Gilbert Wedgecroft. He stood there mum as a maggot. Heaven knows what these doctors can't tell must by glancing at you. Why did he ask me about Ireland? Doesn't he know I never go back?

Trebell   Probably not. We could trust Gilbert.

Amy O'Connell   I don't like him.

Trebell   Why?

Amy O'Connell   Because he doesn't like me, I suppose. He's your friend . . . he'd think of what suited you. I won't

have him told. Give me your word, please, you won't even
hint things to him.

Trebell Very well.

*They are at odds, hopelessly apart; she querulous and distraught, he
considerate, but incapable of soft phrase. Now, though, her voice rises in
the wail of a lost child.*

Amy O'Connell But what am I to do . . . what am I to do?

Trebell There are half a hundred sensible things we can
do . . . when you've steadied your nerves.

Amy O'Connell If only you still loved me a little it would
help! You think I've had lovers . . . besides you. It's not true . .
. whoever has told it you. I've been near enough to the edge of
it. I don't really like men . . . that's the silly thing. But you've
to fool them . . . or they'll fool you. I did do one thing that
wasn't quite right before I was married . . . though nothing
happened. Then Justin wasn't fair to me. He thinks a woman
should sit at home and sew baby-clothes when she's not in
church praying to God to send her a use for them. Still . . .
being a Catholic and confessing now and then does help keep
you straight. Though you can't confess everything. And what
do priests know about marriage anyway? They oughtn't to!
And I'd been getting to be no end of a sceptic and thinking
there might be something in Science and Spiritualism and the
rest. Well . . . I'm punished for that. God lets you be for a bit .
. . and then does something that m a k e s you believe in him. I
nearly went back to Justin to tell him all about it . . . for the
sake of telling someone. But he's queer. He might have killed
me . . . not that I'd mind much. Or he might kill you.

Trebell He'd likelier be off to his lawyer and start a divorce
. . . and remember to be queer and Catholic again when he'd
got it.

Amy O'Connell And that'd smash you.

Trebell At the moment . . . yes.

Amy O'Connell I'd be so sorry. Still . . . you'd marry me.

Trebell   That is the usual thing.

Amy O'Connell   Then you'd hate me the more, I suppose, for being the smashing of you. But we could get along. People do. I'm good company . . . and I'm still pretty. I can't see why you don't love me . . . just a little.

Trebell   I can say that I love you. It's easily said.

Amy O'Connell   You never once said it . . . you'd no need. That's pretty shameful. Did you think I wouldn't notice?

Trebell   It's a sort of lying I dislike . . . using words that have no meaning to me.

Amy O'Connell   Oh, don't talk cleverly now, Henry . . . please! Let's be practical. Tell me what to do.

To these pitiful, ridiculous, revelations what could he find to say? But his own dry – and really rather priggish – piece of pedantry having roused her to a very wholesome impatience, he comes, readily enough, to the bearing of common sense, and, to that extent, of kindness.

Trebell   Well . . . you may count on me for as much of my duty to the child . . . and to you, while the trouble lasts . . . as you'll let me do. My rights are forfeit. That's as it should be . . . the law shows some sense. You can't forfeit yours. A bad time . . . for a few months yet . . . you're bound to have. One or two people must know. If you choose to tell your husband now or later and risk the scandal . . . the rights and the wrongs of that we'd better talk out when you're calmer. But it's your duty, remember . . . whatever else happens . . . to keep yourself fit. And . . . oh, my dear girl! . . . if kindness will do it, I'll be as kind as I know how to be. Well, now . . . you're not tied down . . . you can get off abroad . . . we'll cover your tracks.

Intent on her human needs, he has himself become human; something more than mere kindness and common sense might be rising in him. But she has only listened with a growing horror, her eyes round and staring, her face set; till at last she breaks out, dreadfully . . .

Amy O'Connell   Are you expecting me to go through with this?

Trebell (*echoing*)   . . . Through with it?

Amy O'Connell   I'd sooner kill myself.

He looks at her gravely and speaks gravely.

Trebell   You've got no choice by now, I should suppose, but to go through with it . . . no reasonable choice.

Amy O'Connell   I won't.

Trebell   Put mischievous notions out of your head once and for all.

Amy O'Connell   I'll kill myself sooner.

He is stern, and no kindliness can hide it. She seems to mean precisely what she says.

Trebell   Steady . . . steady! This is the trouble then . . . just this?

You'd not call it a laugh that escapes her.

Amy O'Connell   Yes . . . thank you! . . . just this.

She is suffering; he can still be kind.

Trebell   Try and talk frankly to me. You're not simply afraid?

Amy O'Connell   Why not? I'm ill as it is.

Trebell   Because Nature . . . if you'll let her . . . provides against that, you know. And there's other provision these days. What's at the back of the fear?

To her poor, twisted mind this is mere torture, and she cries out under it.

Amy O'Connell   Oh . . . don't question me . . . and steady me . . . as if I were a beast being broken in! But that's what I am now . . . no better!

Trebell   Come . . . come!

He puts a restraining hand on her. She breaks free and turns on him; desperate, weakly violent.

Amy O'Connell   When I was a girl . . . and no more than a girl . . . I said to myself . . . and I didn't need to say it . . . that never, never, would I have a child.

Trebell   Weren't you foolish, then, to marry?

Amy O'Connell   One has to marry. I was a fool to marry Justin. He found out . . . after a bit. He thinks it's a sin. I said I'd a right to choose. What do women's rights come to if that's not their right? So I left him.

Trebell   But I don't understand your dread.

Amy O'Connell   How should you? Love's beautiful . . . this is beastly. Oh dear, oh dear . . . when I've always been so clever about things that didn't matter much . . . to run up against two such impossible men! No civilised woman wants children growing up around her to remind her she's growing old. If she's trapped into it she makes the best of it . . . or pretends to. Well . . . I won't pretend to. Do you mean to tell me I've no right to choose?

She is growing a little shrill, shedding the daintiness that avails her nothing. Is there something common at the core of her? He grows graver yet.

Trebell   Here's something I've learnt to believe. We choose and we think we've chosen wisely . . . then by some grace we blunder on a better thing. Then comes the test. Have we a sense of it . . . and the faith to go on into the unknown?

Amy O'Connell   A sense of what? Faith! Faith in what?

Trebell   My dear, my dear . . . beauty or brains, what are they worth . . . if we've not enough life in us to pay Life on demand?

Amy O'Connell   I'm in trouble . . . I'm in danger . . . and you talk platitudes to me! Are you going to help me out of this hell or are you not?

Trebell   Through it.

Amy O'Connell   No . . . no . . . no!

Trebell   You'll play no tricks. Mark that now.

Amy O'Connell   Who's to stop me?

Trebell   You'll think of your child.

Amy O'Connell   There's no child . . . and there's not to
be . . . if I say so. And it's my right . . . no one else's to say so.

*What answer can he make? Their anger checked by silence she relapses
into pitifulness again.*

And you've not even said you're sorry . . . you've not even
kissed me. If you loved me just a little I mightn't feel so lost. But
you don't . . . and you never did . . . I knew it all the time. So
I shouldn't believe you now if you said you did. Well . . . I
don't want to lie to you either. What's the use? I daresay I
didn't love you very much . . . once it was over . . . and you'd
gone away.

*These seem to be the depths. But out of them his incorrigible intellect
plucks a forlorn hope.*

Trebell   If that's the truth . . . let's start from that . . .

Amy O'Connell   I don't see what use the truth is. I wish
I were dead.

At this moment the table telephone rings.

Trebell   This'll be Cantilupe.

*He goes to answer. She rises wearily and with something of the indifference
of weariness.*

Amy O'Connell   I've broken up your morning's work . . .
I'm so sorry. The papers have been full of you . . . if I'd needed
reminding of you. You're to save the country . . . or to ruin it.
But somebody's always doing that.

Trebell   He's coming up.

Amy O'Connell   Then for Heaven's sake open the door.

Trebell   Are you going home now . . . back to Charles
Street?

Amy O'Connell   I hadn't thought of it.

*Love her – how can he pretend he does? But he is touched; and to a sort of
reverence for her, little as this is what she asks.*

Trebell   We'll find salvation for you.

Amy O'Connell   Don't mock at me . . . don't cant! You've
done for me . . . isn't that enough? I was happy and free.
You've brought me down and degraded me . . . and what do
you care? I'm nothing to you now. I'm a sick beast . . . unclean
. . . cancerous!

Trebell   Hold your tongue, will you . . . before you believe
what you're saying? You unhappy woman . . . if life only seems
like death to you!

Amy O'Connell   Will you please open that door?

Trebell *opens it and goes out upon the landing. She braces herself –
slips on the mask again – for an encounter with* **Cantilupe**.

Amy O'Connell   Tell Frances I waited in vain for her . . .

Trebell   He's still at the bottom of the stairs.

She takes a last chance to say tensely . . .

Amy O'Connell   Will you find me somebody to go to?

Trebell   No.

Amy O'Connell   Very well, then . . . very well . . . !

Trebell   How are you, Cantilupe?

With this warning to her, **Lord Charles Cantilupe** *appears.*

Cantilupe   I'm a quarter of an hour late. I'm sorry.

Trebell   It's no matter.

Amy O'Connell   I've been distracting him from
statesmanship for ten minutes of it. How do you do and
good-bye!

Cantilupe   A most dangerous distraction.

Amy O'Connell   Sweet of you to say so. Well . . . I leave you to disestablish the Church. I'm sure that between you it'll be beautifully done.

Trebell   Won't you wait . . . for Frances?

Amy O'Connell   What's the use . . . if you're sure she can't help me?

Trebell   I should wait.

Walter Kent *has followed* **Cantilupe** *up the stairs.* **Amy** *strolls across to his room as if she might possibly wait there.*

Amy O'Connell   And this is your kennel? How precious! Dear Frances does spoil you. It's the big room made little. But you must get a pretty cover for your typewriter.

Walter Kent   It's as if the big room had had a baby . . . I'll tell Miss Trebell.

Amy O'Connell   Quite! How witty of you!

Walter, *having made this magnificent gaffe, turns to his chief.*

Walter Kent   Wedgecroft has just sent back a message: will you see him for another moment on his way back to Wimpole Street?

Trebell   Yes.

Walter Kent   Right.

He goes downstairs again. **Amy O'Connell** *stands in the doorway of the little room.* **Trebell** *goes towards her and they are out of* **Cantilupe**'s *sight if not of his hearing.*

Trebell   Please wait for Frances.

Amy O'Connell   I've no faith in any of you.

Trebell   But you'd better wait.

She gives him a little twisted smile, but turns and goes into the room. He closes the door on her and looks as if he'd like to lock it. Then he comes back to **Cantilupe** *and his work, shutting his own door too.*

One sees at once why **Cantilupe** *is nicknamed His Eminence. In spite of his layman's dress – which has besides a dandified individuality about it, permissible, if well contrived, in the man of fifty or over; and* **Cantilupe** *is over – he would be better suited by a purple soutane and red cap, and his face would look well from one of El Greco's canvases. There is a natural, if constrained, courtesy in his speech and movements. He is almost the last man in London to pay old-fashioned compliments to women – and he refers to them as ladies. He has a charming mind and a subtle mind; but he is not a strong man and he knows it; his refuge is in obstinacy. He has the limpid eye of the enthusiast, but the mouth of a fanatic. And he is very wary of* **Trebell.**

Cantilupe   How are you?

Trebell   Very well. How are you?

Cantilupe   A pleasant holiday?

Trebell   Most. A pleasant election?

Cantilupe   The usual thing. Not quite so degrading as usual, perhaps.

After which duellists' parade they settle to what **Cantilupe**, *at any rate, thinks to be a duel.*

Trebell   Well . . . now?

Cantilupe   I've brought you these memoranda back.

Trebell   I hoped you'd keep them.

Cantilupe   My cousin and I have certainly been discussing my possible inclusion in his new Cabinet. But after one turn of office twenty years ago I had made up my mind against another.

Trebell   Why . . . if that's not too personal a question?

Cantilupe   No. I find myself inevitably at war with the master-fallacy of a godless age . . . the belief that the things

we do can be better . . . or other . . . than the thing we are.
I distrust most modern legislation, that is to say.

Trebell (*appreciative but practical*)   But you'd sooner have
something to say to this Disestablishment business . . . if it's got
to be.

Cantilupe   Oh, I'm for it . . . reluctantly . . . Church and
State Tory though I remain at least. But as the modern State
hardly reflects my heart's desire, I have come to think that the
Church can best serve it . . . and best save her own soul . . . by
breaking partnership.

Trebell   Well . . . I hope you'll be in the Cabinet.

Cantilupe   Horsham told me you hoped so. It was a surprise
to me.

Trebell   Till you read my memoranda.

Cantilupe   I never expected a scheme of yours to seem so
favourable to my point of view.

Trebell   Could you do better for your section of the Church
with a Bill of your own?

Cantilupe   Not so well, as I'm sure you know. 'Section' I
protest against. My friends and I are for the Church and the
whole Church as we conceive the Church. But an appearance
of sectionalism has been thrust on us . . . and whatever we
might propose would excite prejudice. I doubt my use in a
Cabinet anyway . . . I detest intrigue. I might do more for my
own people . . . and for you even . . . by supporting your Bill
from the back benches. Frankly, Mr Trebell . . . I want to
know why you want me on the front one.

Trebell   You want to know that I'm not drafting a Bill to
bring you into the Cabinet . . . so that once you're in I may
back down upon every item of it while I keep you in . . . till
I've so bedevilled your influence that it won't much matter
whether you're out or in. For you're a danger on the back
benches . . . even as I was. No . . . those are the policies by
which we perish. But you see me at best, I suppose, as a sceptic

lawyer, content if he can fence you all with your controversies into some form of words and not caring if you starve there. No. Again, no. You're wrong, believe me . . . though it's a safe start to think the worst of any man. I want you with me because you believe in your Church. And though I've to disestablish I'm not out to destroy. I hate all destruction.

Cantilupe   I do believe you . . . and I beg your pardon.

Trebell *has won the first bout, evidently.*

Trebell   Thank you. Well . . . what will you examine me on? Appropriation . . . ? Buildings . . . ?

Cantilupe   There'll be a lot of silly sentiment to combat over Buildings.

Trebell   Yes. These idolaters of Art!

Cantilupe   Will you show me one of them that cares a rap what goes on inside the church after he has preserved it?

Trebell   No . . . they'll be a nuisance. Representation . . . pre-Restoration endowments?

Cantilupe *is fingering through the memoranda,* **Trebell** *has the whole thing in his head.*

Cantilupe   The figures there are troublesome.

Trebell   Very rough figures so far.

Cantilupe   Your solution of the country parish problem would make a good election cry. Ten square miles and a thousand a year for a curate and a car!

Trebell   It's mainly a question of locomotion. I don't much like the Rural District options though.

Cantilupe   And your disputed surplus to go to Education?

Trebell   Yes.

Cantilupe   That's the heart of the plan.

Trebell   The very heart of it.

Cantilupe   It sounds well. And the more we quarrel over the loaves and fishes the more Education may get?

Trebell   Do you object?

Cantilupe   It asks a little courage to object. But every big Bill in my time has had its one provision which the press would unite to praise and all parties promise to support . . . in principle . . . upon a first reading. Yet it seldom survived Committee. I have wondered if it ever was meant to. Not quite perversely, I have sometimes opposed it from the start.

Trebell   I shall stand by the education proposals.

Cantilupe   Or fall?

Trebell   I don't think I shall fall by them.

Cantilupe   Well . . . nor do I! So I've been prying into them pretty sharply.

Trebell   I supposed you would.

It is genial cut and thrust – though 'genial', perhaps, is hardly the word of either of them. But they are getting on splendidly.

Cantilupe   It comes to this. You think the old quarrel over the children is too dead to blaze up again over the teachers?

Trebell   Things have changed. Things do change. We've learnt a little. We do learn by being brayed in the mortar of experience. I'd have been on your side in the old quarrel. Atmosphere in a school or college . . . why, it's what most matters. The first thing a child must learn is that he lives by faith. One and one makes two, don't they, by God's grace . . . I'm told there's no other proof. If we could have done with textbook teachers . . . ! But there are never enough good men to go round . . . that's the perennial trouble in this over-engined civilisation. We've to put our money into finding and training them, though.

Cantilupe   How many of these colleges do you think your surplus will run to?

Trebell Fifty, I hope . . . more or less. I don't want 'em too big. And I mean to house them when I can . . . though we needn't give this away yet . . . in the country seat that the country gentleman can't sit in any longer. You're not enough of a Tory for me, Cantilupe. You were mourning last Budget over the sad fate of the big country houses. Won't it comfort you to see an abbey or two turned back after four centuries' usurpation to something of the use it was meant for?

This is fascinating, no doubt; but **Cantilupe** *follows his trail.*

Cantilupe And the Church colleges will be under Church control?

Trebell Yes . . . I'll find the money elsewhere for the secular . . . and some of the undenominational . . . balance. There's a good lump being released . . . and a lot of slack to take up.

Cantilupe *here puts down the memoranda.*

Cantilupe Would you let me ask you, Mr Trebell . . . though I'm aware that in these days the question's thought almost an indecent one . . . what is your own attitude towards my Church?

Trebell I'd like you to know. I grew up in the late nineteenth-century, neo-Polytechnic belief that you couldn't take God seriously and be an FRS. And when I'd done wanting to be an Admiral of the Fleet and the engine-driver of the Scotch Express I wanted to be an FRS. For there were my father's books on the top shelves. He'd sold his ambitions for domesticity and a dispensary practice in West Croydon. But he died of it . . . and I foreswore poverty. Later . . . in a certain loneliness of heart . . . I began to go to church again. I didn't want to be preached at. But I did want to feel myself . . . amid week-day battlings for success . . . one of the congregation of faithful men. I'd read to the end of my prayer-book, you perceive. And after all it was m y Church as by law established. But that didn't last.

Cantilupe What lost you to us?

Trebell Intellectual conscience. I can't take your sacraments. I can't say your creeds. I've tried . . . I don't believe them. You do?

Cantilupe Certainly I do.

Trebell Damned odd you should! Without reserve?

Cantilupe With no reserve.

Trebell I can respect that. Save me from Mr Facing-both-ways. The present may be his . . . but never the future.

Cantilupe You are to set my Church free to save herself from him.

Trebell Quite so. But when that's done . . . what will you do for me and for men of my kind in return? Churchmen at heart . . . members one of another in science or statecraft . . . with no use at all for conventicles and their self-righteousness. Nor even for the promise of salvation hereafter . . . for we die pretty tired, most of us. But with much need to sanctify here on earth the world of power that our secular minds have made.

Cantilupe I have found it, I fear, to be a world of intellectual pride . . . with many simpler lessons still to learn.

Of a sudden he is on his defence, acrid and aloof. **Trebell** *breaks out in good-tempered exasperation . . .*

Trebell Heavens above! Even now you don't repent?

Cantilupe Of what?

Trebell Of these . . . how many? . . . generations of the loss of us . . . of the men who've made the world as it is.

Cantilupe As it is! As it is!!

Trebell The while your Church has been a squabbling ground for third-rate minds . . . most of them; come now! . . . fighting unreal issues into such confusion that at last all parties only want to be quit of you!

Cantilupe You are hardly refuting my accusation of arrogance.

Trebell Our issue's joined, then. Well . . . do you run away?

They are on good terms again. **Cantilupe** *takes up the memoranda to emphasise his disclaimer.*

Cantilupe No.

Trebell Good. Then let's get the issue clear. The Establishment has been your fortress . . . but it has been your prison too.

Cantilupe I admit it. Well . . . a living faith need not fear freedom.

Trebell Nor learning for its own sake?

Cantilupe Nor learning, certainly!

Trebell Very well. The statutes for your colleges are going to be the test of that. And I'll not be afraid of your faith and its dogmas either. Admit with me that hunger for knowledge is a spiritual hunger and its balking or its warping a sin against the light . . . and I ask no more of you.

> 'On a huge hill
> Cragged and steep Truth stands, and he that will
> Reach her, about must, and about must go.'

Cantilupe *is really delighted.*

Cantilupe Donne!

Trebell The poet, wasn't he, of your Church's last great dilemma? I believe in your Church too, you see . . . all apart from what your Church may believe in . . . and in more Churches than one. For I believe in vocation . . . in the calling of voices from that hill, however confusedly. I dislike trade . . . the shrewd mind . . . the measuring of profit . . . and property in toil. The world's great ages have had strength to spare and to waste. And even the waste . . . imaginings, art, adventures . . . was fruitful. The fruit of it is ours today. You promise men in

their poverty a future life. Why not make them the fight of
it now? That's no paradox. Once we're through with youth's
appetites and illusions, what does our carnal life hold for us?
The past becomes a picture-book. The moment as it passes
can't be very interesting . . . saving your presence . . . for we
live it ignobly chained. But the future! That we create . . .
selflessly . . . out of ourselves. We can be honourably happy
there. And what wise creator will want to know too much
about his creation? I have strange visions of your churches,
Cantilupe . . . and of week-day praises to God. Of cathedral
cloisters busy with dispute. And of every parson in the country
turned scholar and schoolmaster . . . with his soul really set
upon eternal things. What a chance for you now . . . what a
chance! And it may be a last chance . . . so I'm out to make
you take it. You shall give us in your freedom what you denied
us in your fetters. You shan't leave any longer the world's
powers and the men that wield them to the anarchy of unbelief.
It may be our civilisation's last chance too. You Churchmen
shall write us a creed for our children to believe. You shall
sanctify their new world for them or perish.

Though he is still speaking to **Cantilupe** *he has, in a sense, ceased to
speak to him. There is silence for a moment.*

Cantilupe   If my invitation stands and I join the Cabinet,
it will be for the pleasure of hearing you propound this Bill to
them.

There is ever such a touch of irony in the compliment. **Trebell** *responds
to it.*

Trebell   Not in these terms!

Cantilupe   No . . . perhaps not. And you'll have some not
too nice bargains to drive, I fear, in and out of Cabinet.

Trebell   That's all in a day's work. But I needed another sort
of understanding with you. Ah . . . you wanted my coat, did
you, Cantilupe? You shall have my cloak also. You'd have me
go with you a mile? By Jove, you shall go with me twain!

Their conference is breaking up. **Cantilupe** *has risen. He is, one remarks, taking the memoranda away with him again.*

Cantilupe   We'll go very willingly, I assure you, as far as we find we can go. Your heresy, Mr Trebell, has its fascinations . . . as other such heresies have had. We can't burn you, nowadays . . . we must try to profit by you.

Trebell   Yes. The blood of the martyrs you've made . . . that also has been the seed of the Church.

Trebell *has given of his best – for he felt the need – to win* **Cantilupe**. *But it is hard to say how far he has succeeded.*

Cantilupe   The Church's wisdom has been to know how much, on the whole, may be expected of men. And the hells of this world are paved, don't you think, less with good intentions than with high ideals.

Trebell *laughs: it is a shrewd hit for a finish. He takes from his table the papers that* **Horsham** *returned him.*

Trebell   Here are more Appropriation figures . . . no, I'd like to put these tidy. I can show you a draft of the Fabrics scheme in a few days.

Cantilupe (*his eye twinkling coldly*)   And of those statutes?

Trebell   I'd like another talk first.

Cantilupe   Could you lunch with me . . . on Thursday?

Trebell   Yes. We must find out our differences. Hullo!

They have moved to the door and **Trebell** *has opened it. There stands* **Wedgecroft**, *watch in hand. And one sees that the door of the little room is open.*

Wedgecroft   I was giving you two minutes more. (*To* **Cantilupe**.) How are you?

Cantilupe   Is Brampton better?

Wedgecroft   Much. I've just been in to see him.

Cantilupe   Good-bye.

Abruptly, as is his habit, he departs. **Wedgecroft** *strolls towards the fire.* **Trebell,** *seeing* **Cantilupe** *down the stairs, is alive to the little room's open door. He goes in quickly to make sure the room is empty; then, but not quite as quickly, he comes out again.*

Trebell   Been here long? I'm sorry.

Wedgecroft   No. No . . . not long. Converted His Eminence, have you?

Trebell   I shall yet.

Wedgecroft   The sight of him might explain why the early Christians took a fish for their symbol.

Trebell   Did you see Mrs O'Connell?

Wedgecroft   On her way out.

Trebell   She was waiting for Frances. Is she coming back?

Wedgecroft   She didn't say. By the way . . . is she a Catholic?

Trebell   He is.

Wedgecroft   Ever met him?

Trebell   No.

Wedgecroft   I knew him at Balliol. When he came into Irish money and land he thought it his duty to go back and live there. Then he went Republican. Does she see much of him?

Trebell   Not more than she can help, I think.

Neither **Trebell,** *nor, be it noted,* **Wedgecroft,** *have seemed quite ingenuous in this little talk.*

Trebell   Well . . . what about Brampton?

Wedgecroft   Will you go and see him?

Trebell   When?

Wedgecroft   Now.

Trebell (*his look is dark, his thoughts are away*)   No, I can't. Yes .. . I could.

Wedgecroft   Then you'd better. He wants me to order him to Scotland tomorrow. He wanted me to order him pork pie and old Marsala for lunch. For God's sake give him something . . . a little more digestible . . . to occupy his m i n d. You've messed up my whole morning, Henry. Curse you . . . and farewell.

Trebell   Sorry!

Wedgecroft   You're not. My patients may die in dozens . . . what would you care? Hullo, young woman!

This last is evidently to someone unseen by us, whom he meets on the stairs. He is gone. **Trebell**, *left alone for a moment, his face still dark and thoughtful, fingers the telephone, then discards it as useless and sits down to write a note.* **Lucy Davenport** *appears on the landing and stands looking from one room to the other.* **Trebell**, *conscious of interruption, glances up.*

Lucy Davenport   No . . . please!

Trebell   D'you want your young man . . . my young man .. . our young man? He's on an errand.

Lucy Davenport   He's back . . . paying his cab.

Trebell   Taking him out to lunch?

Lucy Davenport   May I?

Trebell   Do.

He has gone back to the writing of his note. **Walter Kent** *comes upstairs and turns into his own room, saying . . .*

Walter Kent   You've no right up here. Go and hide. You'll get me the sack.

Trebell   Walter!

Walter Kent   Sir?

Trebell   Ring for a messenger boy.

Walter Kent   Right!

Trebell *finishes his note and has only the envelope to address.*

Trebell   But I wish you'd get married, you two . . . and have done with it.

Lucy Davenport   I have named the day. We're to be the first pair tied up by your Disestablished Church. Or shall I put it off? I've come to tell you I will. For two years. And I'll go to India and come back by Japan . . . the Tyrrells have asked me to. I sent him on his holiday with you . . . that was a pledge of good faith. But if you're still so sure I'm a nuisance I'll get right out of the way.

Trebell *looks up, a little touched.* **Walter** *has come out of his room and the two stand together in the doorway, a very wholesomely happy pair.*

Trebell   He'd only fret for you. D'you hear this?

Walter Kent   I'm not sure I want to marry her anyhow. She takes me too seriously. I shall never go the pace. But she'd make you the perfect secretary.

Lucy Davenport   I tried for that once . . . through Miss Trebell . . . when I thought you no longer loved me. He wouldn't look at me. But I'll make y o u a perfect secretary.

Walter Kent   Well . . . !

Trebell   Run along! The Saumarez appointment's at two?

Walter Kent   Quarter past. I'll be back.

They go happily downstairs together. **Trebell** *seals his envelope, his face still very dark.*

Act Three

Horsham's *drawing-room in Queen Anne's Gate, with its soft grey walls, its mellow old French carpet and furniture, its spare and formal decoration, is a fit setting for the man himself, mellow of mind, classic in his tastes, his emotions faded, of a temper sceptical and fastidious. He is standing at this moment before a noiseless fire (he dislikes noise, and the very fires in his house, even as the servants that lay and light them, seem to have learnt to conform), his head bent, his benign brow wrinkled in perplexity. If he glances up he sees on the sofa in front of him* **Wedgecroft,** *who, though it is late, is still wearing the regulation kit of his busy doctor's day, and is sitting there, nervously irritable – as he seldom is – and depressed. With his back to them both, on a sofa with its back to them, is* **George Farrant,** *knees apart, hands clasped, head bent, very glum.* **Horsham** *glances beyond him to the big double doors of the library and to the door on the left of them that leads to the passage, as if either of them might open to admit an expected visitor. And, if his gaze travels back along the room, it passes over the long black piano ranged against the wall to where, poised on the music bench, as if it were a stool of repentance, is* **Lord Charles Cantilupe.** *His face is grave and set, but calm. The general air of the conclave, however, suggests a problem discussed and discussed and yet unsolved. It is, in fact, a charged silence that* **Farrant** *breaks by asking irritably . . .*

Farrant   But what time did you ask him to come, Horsham?

Horsham   O'Connell?

Farrant   Yes . . . we're talking of O'Connell, aren't we?

Horsham (*pacifically*)   Did you give him a specific time, Wedgecroft?

Wedgecroft   Not before half-past ten, I told him.

Farrant (*eyeing his watch*)   Twenty to eleven . . . just.

Wedgecroft   He'll come.

Farrant   Blackborough's not turning up, though.

Horsham   He was dining at Coombe . . . I sent a note after him.

Cantilupe   Saumarez caught me by mere chance, Cyril . . . I was off to Tonbridge by the 10.15. I happened to go home for some papers.

The little eddy of this talk dies down. Then **Horsham**, *in bland recognition of the irony of life's happenings (his first apprehension of them is always of their irony, his blandness in the face of it seems never to fail him) . . .*

Horsham   And I interned O'Connell during the Rebellion, did I?

Wedgecroft   You did.

Horsham   Surely . . . surely he has no grievance against me because of that!

Cantilupe   But . . . Mrs O'Connell being dead . . . what is to precipitate the scandal?

Cantilupe *was a late arrival, evidently.* **Horsham** *gives him the necessary facts, cut and dry.*

Horsham   The inquest.

Cantilupe   Which can't be avoided?

Horsham   It seems not.

Cantilupe   Tomorrow?

Horsham   Tomorrow.

Wedgecroft *breaks out.*

Wedgecroft   Good God! . . . I'd have risked the police-court and given the certificate if she'd died right away . . . and I thought she was gone that evening she sent for me. But O'Connell, when he came, said: 'Call in old Fielding Andrews.' I couldn't object.

Horsham   How much had Sir Fielding to be told?

Wedgecroft   Not about Trebell, of course.

Horsham   But the yet more unpleasant part of the business . . .

Wedgecroft   Heavens! . . . if I'd left him to find that out
he'd have suspected m e. And he'd have found out. He's half
blind and three-quarters deaf . . . but there's not much he
misses. Well . . . I might have risked it . . .

Farrant   Oh, my dear fellow . . . quixotic!

Wedgecroft   . . . but whoever the quack was she did go to . . .
the police may be on his track . . . the whole thing might have
come out that way . . . and then where should I have been?

Farrant   I suppose . . . even now . . . there's no getting hold
of the Coroner?

Farrant, *Privy Councillor though he is, speaks for the moment as might
a village schoolboy of robbing an orchard.* **Horsham** *is very definite on
this point. And when he is definite upon a question – he seldom seems to
be – he sings a little song . . .*

Horsham   No, no! No, no, no! No, no, no, no!

Farrant   Brampton thought we'd better try.

This offers a pleasant opening.

Horsham   He would think so! I admire Brampton . . . I have
even had moments of liking for Brampton . . . and I have been
in four Cabinets with him. But for flippancy of mind . . . and
for perversity of conduct . . . in great matters as in small . . . he
is unsurpassed.

Cantilupe   Was he quite too ill to come tonight?

Farrant   He said Wedgecroft wouldn't hear of it.

Wedgecroft   True! I didn't hear of it.

Horsham   Was it necessary, then, to confide in him? He's
the greatest gossip in London. The one pleasure life has left
him – apart from bullying Her Ladyship – being his scabrous
little chats with the dozen or so young women whom he
honours with his senile attentions!

If **Horsham** *were an old woman — and his opponents have been known to call him so — he might, one fears, be accounted a cat. But, really, this is an exceptional outburst. His temper at the moment is seriously tried. He must keep his serenity for the business in hand. A little snappishness is a safety-valve. Still, one sees well enough why his colleagues do not court the rough side of his tongue.* **Farrant**'s *own crest falls a little.*

Farrant   Leave nothing undone, I thought . . .

Horsham   Even the unwise thing! You may be right. Sometimes one's very errors conspire to help one. Try the Coroner if you like!

Farrant   No . . . I admit I don't fancy being snubbed by a Coroner.

Wedgecroft *rather roughly brings the talk back to the point.*

Wedgecroft   Besides . . . this man's keen on these cases. He had one last year he kept adjourning till they did nab the culprit. And the *Mail* wrote leaders and reported him verbatim. There's a lot of birth-control propaganda in his district. That has his back up.

Cantilupe   Small wonder!

There is cold passion in his voice as he says this. Two subjects so rouse him — birth-control and vivisection — and he does not argue about them.

Wedgecroft   He's a Plymouth Brother.

Cantilupe (*disappointed*)   Really! But that's not right either.

Horsham (*his eyes upturned to the classic Adam ceiling*)   Why do not the members of that distressful sect abandon a designation which does so suggest gin-drinking?

Wedgecroft (*forcibly*)   You're at O'Connell's mercy . . . that's what it comes to. If he doesn't keep a guard on his tongue, there'll be an adjournment . . . and the whole story will be out. I've said all I can say to him . . . so has Farrant. If this conclave can't impress him . . . Trebell's done for.

Cantilupe   Did she confess to her husband?

Wedgecroft   I don't think she opened her mouth from the time he came till she died. But he found a letter Trebell wrote her . . . ten days ago . . . on her table. She'd never had it.

Horsham   A letter! I ask you! Here's a lawyer and a man of the world . . . in a situation of this sort . . . writes the woman a letter!

Wedgecroft   It wouldn't have meant much . . . apart from the catastrophe.

Horsham (*fatherly, grandfatherly, quite patriarchal*)   My dear Wedgecroft . . . when trouble begins . . . political or personal . . . write one letter only . . . the one that you know will get you safe out of it. And let that be a short one.

Wedgecroft   Anyhow . . . once she was dead he told me to tell O'Connell the whole truth. And I had to . . . or he'd have gone himself to tell him. I had to stop that somehow.

Cantilupe   Mrs O'Connell consulted you first of all . . . did you say?

Wedgecroft   I met her at Trebell's just by chance . . . last Thursday week it was . . . the day he got back from abroad.

Cantilupe (*gravely*)   I was there.

Wedgecroft   Were you? So you were.

Horsham   You met her at Trebell's . . . at Trebell's!

Farrant   She was friends with Frances.

Horsham   Frances?

Farrant   His sister.

Wedgecroft   By the way . . . Frances knows nothing yet.

Horsham   Ah . . . yes! An exceptional woman . . . a modestly intelligent woman!

Wedgecroft   She tackled me . . . saved her face by a few lies . . . and asked me plump to help her out. I told her I couldn't . . . I knew there was no excuse. Oh . . . there are men who would have on one pretext or another.

Horsham   Really! Reputable men?

Wedgecroft   I believe you gave one of 'em a knighthood.

He's not sorry for the chance of a dig at **Horsham.** **Horsham** *is horrified.*

Horsham   Surely not!

Wedgecroft   No . . . it wasn't you.

Horsham   But are these practices known to their colleagues?

Wedgecroft   Oh, my dear Horsham! When I retire . . . if you're in office . . . I shall write you an open letter entitled 'How Not to Organise the Medical Profession'.

Horsham   Please don't! What unkindness have I ever done you? Please, my dear Wedgecroft, don't!

Wedgecroft   I suppose I might have sent her to one of them . . . and I wish I had now. Then if things had gone wrong she'd have died in the odour of sanctified science . . . and there'd have been an end of that.

Cantilupe   Where did she go?

Wedgecroft   I've no notion.

Cantilupe   Who did send her?

Wedgecroft   I've no idea. She bolted out of sight and knowledge for a week . . . without even a maid . . . to some dirty little country lodging. That's what put her in the cart. Then she dragged herself back with a temperature of a hundred and three . . . and sent for me. Even then she didn't tell me the full facts. So when O'Connell came I spoke to him quite openly. All he said was that it wouldn't have been his child.

Trebell *and their own troubles vanish from their minds for a moment.*

Farrant   Poor devil!

Horsham   Poor woman!

Farrant   There's one thing more you might make clear,
Wedgecroft . . . that Trebell didn't even know of her going to
this quack.

Wedgecroft   She'd threatened to go . . . he was trying to
stop her. His letter shows that. She disappeared . . . he was
trying to find her . . .

Farrant   Otherwise I'd not be lifting a finger to save him.

Horsham   How long have you known O'Connell, George?

Farrant   I was with him at Harrow . . . we found together.
I've hardly seen him since. And I wouldn't have spoken to him
now . . . after what he did in the Rebellion . . . but for this.

Horsham   Oh . . . why? Still, I wish I hadn't interned him.

Cantilupe   But may I ask, Cyril, why I am here?

Before **Horsham** *can answer,* **Saumarez,** *his secretary, comes quietly
from the library.* **Saumarez** *is a man of forty. He has abandoned a
normally distinguished career in the Civil Service out of devotion to*
Horsham *and from a dislike of routine. In his spare moments – he has
few – he walks disinterestedly in the more removed paths of literature.*

Saumarez   Mr O'Connell's come.

Horsham   In there, is he?

Saumarez   Will you see him alone, first?

Horsham   I think not. And do go home now, Saumarez.
You've had a long day . . . and two hours of it with your dentist!

Saumarez   I'm all right, sir. Besides, what about
Blackborough? You must be pretty tired yourself.

He returns to the library.

Horsham   I a m very tired. I left Lympne at seven this
morning . . . I've been at it ever since. I read the whole Nigeria
report on the way up . . . I detest reading in a car.

Cantilupe   Cyril . . . what is m y position . . . ?

Horsham   Shh!

For the library door has opened and **Saumarez**'s *voice can be heard saying 'Mr O'Connell, sir'. And* **Justin O'Connell** *comes in. He is a man, as we have just heard, of Farrant's age, but he looks older; an Irish gentleman and scholar, and no foreigner could look more foreign among these Englishmen than he does. His face is lined by more than thought, by intellectual passion. A man capable of devotion and of suffering, but not, one would say, of happiness. Whatever his thoughts or feelings are now, however, they are masked in a frigid, formal politeness.* **Horsham**, *sensitive to this, subdues his welcome and his introductions to tonelessness.*

Horsham   How do you do? Let me see . . . do you know my cousin, Charles Cantilupe? Farrant? . . . yes. We are still expecting Russell Blackborough. Sir Henry Brampton is ill. Do sit down.

O'Connell *does so; and the rest re-settle themselves – all but* **Wedgecroft**, *who in the ensuing pause says, half aloud, to* **Horsham** . . .

Wedgecroft   I could wait a bit for Blackborough and tell him all he need know. That'll free Saumarez. Then you won't want me again.

Horsham   Thank you so much.

O'Connell   If you're not still busy at this hour, Dr Wedgecroft, would you perhaps wait a few minutes also for me? . . . but a very few, I think, it will need to be.

Wedgecroft   All right.

This little speech of **O'Connell**'s *only deepens the chill with which his very appearance affected the gathering; and* **Wedgecroft**'s *intentionally off-hand response as he passes into the library does nothing to lift it. Yet another silence follows;* **Horsham** *is still feeling his way. But* **O'Connell** *himself breaks it.*

O'Connell   You sent for me, Horsham.

This allows the pleasantest of responses, which comes promptly and charmingly.

Horsham   My message gave you, I hope, no impression of being sent for.

But charm he never so wisely, **Horsham** *will charm here in vain.*

O'Connell   As an Irishman I am happily less concerned nowadays to know by what persons, in or out of office, this country is governed. Very well . . . you did not send for me. But I am here.

Horsham   And you know what we have to ask you.

O'Connell   I think I do. Farrant and Wedgecroft at least have not spared energy in impressing upon me that if this man's adultery with my wife becomes as notorious tomorrow as its consequences for her are to be . . . public opinion may make it hard for you to add him to your government.

Horsham   Public opinion . . . so called . . . so called! . . . would, rightly or wrongly, but quite unfailingly, oust him from public life for some years to come at least.

O'Connell   It is your business to be aware of such things.

Horsham *now faces his task.*

Horsham   Mr O'Connell . . . a great wrong has been done you . . . and no one here will say a word to excuse it. Nor have we any title to ask your forgiveness for the guilty man. But for the reputation . . . and so for the very existence . . . not of the man, but of the statesman, I am prepared to plead with you . . . and I do.

But **O'Connell** *will have none of these subtleties either.*

O'Connell   My wife is dead. For Mr Trebell . . . I do not know the man . . . in the statesman I am uninterested. But I am to cover their sin tomorrow . . . am I . . . with a lie?

This is really rather brutal, and **Farrant** *brings good British common sense into the account.*

Farrant   No . . . you won't have to lie as far as I can see. The Coroner must keep his questions within bounds. Well . . . you'll have to lie by implication. In a good cause! So that won't imperil your mortal soul, I take it.

O'Connell *turns to him with grave disdain.*

O'Connell   Our souls are in constant peril. That is not troubling me.

Farrant   Well, what is the worry then? I've talked myself to a standstill with you. So has Wedgecroft. We've not found out.

O'Connell   No? It was not the way, perhaps.

Irony is lost on **Farrant***: the more credit to his good heart.*

Farrant   I haven't excused Trebell . . . I'm not defending that sort of thing. There's the old sign still stuck up: Trespassers will be prosecuted. Mostly they're not. If the game amuses you . . . you run the risk. But no one expects this sort of consequence. If you won't think of his reputation . . . think of your wife's. Why make a perfectly unprofitable mess of things now?

It does not occur to dear **Farrant** *that to talk himself to a standstill yet again will be profitless; it does, however, to* **Horsham***.*

Horsham   May we hear your difficulties, please, Mr O'Connell . . . if you think we can help you in them?

Cantilupe *breaks silence, pale-voiced.*

Cantilupe   May I just say, Cyril . . . all, I think, that I shall want to say. You are a Catholic, I believe, Mr O'Connell . . . you are a Christian gentleman. Trebell will have need of your forgiveness. I cannot tell you he is asking it . . . and we are told (*a glance at* **Horsham**) we have no right to. He may yet be thinking . . . even as we seem to be . . . of less profitable things. But . . . after God's forgiveness . . . he will need yours. And if you forgive him you will know better than we whether you should then save him from such clumsy vengeance as this world takes.

For the first time a little life stirs in **O'Connell***'s face.*

O'Connell   You are an apt advocate, Lord Charles.

From the library comes **Mr Blackborough***, businesslike as usual, but too businesslike to emphasise his interruption needlessly.*

Horsham   Ah! You've met Russell Blackborough?

O'Connell   No.

Blackborough   How d'you do?

Horsham   . . . who joins us, I'm sure, in this appeal to you.

Blackborough   Heartily. I've seen Wedgecroft.

When one says 'Heartily' with such convinced gravity but with so little heartiness as that, one means to imply that really the matter is too near one's heart for easy emotional expression. With **Blackborough***, of course, this may be so. He sits, with equal conviction, in the nearest chair.* **Horsham***, now gently dominating, proceeds . . .*

Horsham   And . . . to sum up . . . with forty years of public life to look back upon . . . I have seen men come and I have seen them go . . . but I do not remember a career of more potent promise than is Trebell's at this moment. A certain eccentricity of attitude may have hampered him so far. But office with its exigencies will cure that. I approached him upon this Disestablishment question last July with much misgiving, I confess. But his reduction of the problem – fraught, as we know, with the passions of centuries – to practical terms has so far been more than remarkable. Talent for politics is not uncommon. Genius is rare . . . how rare! I do not hesitate to say that I discern it in Trebell. Your country needs him, Mr O'Connell. My country, then . . . if you, unhappily, now count yourself a stranger here. What more can I say?

With another man the unfortunate anti-climax would have spoiled the whole effect. But **Horsham** *has a way of making even his blunders effective, by investing his recovery from them with an appealing, helpless charm. Yet* **O'Connell** *shows no response and* **Farrant** *has another simple try.*

Farrant   Oh . . . be a good fellow. Come!

And now they definitely wait for his reply.

O'Connell   Do I seem stubborn? I'm sorry . . . it is not quite that. But I am now a stranger to your time as to your country, Horsham . . . . and such talk as this means nothing to me. I have chosen for my refuge a century in which men had to have the courage even of their sins . . . and my statecraft has been studied under the fi r s t Edward.

Horsham (*so comprehending*)   Yes . . . yes, indeed. And only the other day, in a little address I had to make at Gray's Inn, I referred to that remarkable chapter upon the Confirmatio Cartarum . . .

O'Connell, *it is to be regretted, quite ignores this compliment.*

O'Connell   What, then, are your politics to me? And, if you must rouse me from my indifference to you . . . better think, perhaps, what you may rouse.

Farrant   I know! You're a Republican . . . you hate the lot of us . . . we're your Saxon oppressors . . .

O'Connell   I am not a Republican . . . . Nor any other sort of lunatic. But it was just possible, Farrant, to prefer the folly and passion of my own people to the sloven good humour which is the boast of yours. Yes, you can rouse me to hate you . . . for all you do . . . and for what you are. And the hate will come from beyond me . . . so that I will be justified of it.

Farrant *can endure it no longer. He flings out of his chair.*

Farrant   O'Connell . . . I'm sorry for your trouble. But what you're talking about now I'm damned if I know. This conversation had better finish without me.

Horsham   Patience . . . George . . . !

Farrant   No, if it gratifies him to wreck Trebell's career and put your government in Queer Street . . . let him. He can. Good God Almighty!

This last exclamation springs form him as he opens the library door for escape; and it seems to have nothing to do with his main protest – though it just might have. But he does not escape. On the contrary he shuts the door again quickly.

Cantilupe   What's the matter?

Farrant   Nothing. Go ahead. I'll hold my tongue. I'll try to.

He sits down incontinently. **Cantilupe** *had wondered for a moment if he felt ill.* **Horsham***, however, calmly continues . . .*

Horsham   Mr O'Connell will not yield, I am sure, to any such vulgar temptation.

Cantilupe   But what is it you hate in us, may I ask, Mr O'Connell?

O'Connell   What . . . when even you can speak to me of forgiveness as if it were a penny in my pocket . . . and a ransom for him from the jealous and ignorant mob that you've made your masters!

As incontinently **Farrant** *gets up again and vanishes into the library.* **Horsham** *is growing a little fretful.*

Horsham   Whatever is the matter with George?

O'Connell   This clever fellow with his clever scheme! Is the fate of the two of them worth a lie? For your time breeds such – and will – till its corruption burst. You might better thank me to rid you . . .

Once again the library door is opened, this time with a sort of violent difficulty. There might be a tussle taking place. There is; though it is an all but noiseless one. In a second the result of it is evident. **Trebell** *stands in the doorway, and* **Farrant** *behind him, rather dishevelled. The assembly is speechless; well it may be. But* **O'Connell** *and* **Trebell** *himself seem the least concerned.* **Trebell** *speaks at last and casually enough.*

Trebell   Forgive me, Horsham, for thrusting myself in. Wedgecroft did his best. Sorry, I've wrecked your collar.

This over his shoulder to **Farrant***, who proceeds to adjust it. A collar escaped from its stud would discompose an archangel.* **O'Connell** *is now standing isolated facing* **Trebell***, who faces him full.*

O'Connell   You are the man?

Trebell   Yes.

O'Connell   Better we should meet.

Trebell   Simpler. I thought so.

Farrant   For God's sake, Trebell . . . come away!

Trebell   What's happening?

Horsham   Mr O'Connell . . . how Trebell knew of your presence here I can't say. No one of us, I'm sure, is responsible for t h i s.

Trebell   You're begging me off. Is that the way?

Farrant   This isn't.

The two ignore the rest. They might be alone together. The Irish voice keeps its level irony.

O'Connell   What then can I do for you?

Trebell   What she was to you . . . you know. Tell the truth of it tomorrow. She has had to die to trap me. I'll tell the truth of that if need be.

If no one else understands, **O'Connell** *does; and he blazes into a white fire of passion.*

O'Connell   Yes, indeed . . . yes, indeed . . . a worthless woman! Had she borne you your child I could better have forgiven her. She could cheat me of mine and leave me. Is the curse of barrenness to be nothing to a man? God forgive her now. What have I left to forgive? I think we are brothers in misfortune, sir. (*Then, as an afterthought, and as if grown aware of the rest.*) I shall say nothing tomorrow that will compromise Mr Trebell.

A silence; then, as no one else will, **Horsham** *has to speak.*

Horsham   Thank you. Each one of us thanks you, I'm sure . . . for your magnanimity.

Cantilupe   Thank you.

Blackborough   Most magnanimous.

Farrant   Good fellow . . . I knew you would be!

Horsham   Thank you . . . once again, thank you.

Trebell, *be it noted, has not thanked him. Instead, and with a queer edge upon his voice, he says . . .*

Trebell   So all's well. And I'm to go ahead, am I, Horsham? I'd like to know.

Farrant   Why not?

Trebell   It's what I came about.

Horsham   You feel . . . I hope . . . under every obligation to go ahead.

Trebell   If you say so.

Farrant   But what's the trouble.

Trebell   What do you say, Blackborough?

Blackborough *sees his drift. So does* **Cantilupe**, *but he is silent. So does* **Horsham**, *but he'd ignore it.* **Farrant** *soon begins to and refuses to.* **O'Connell**, *motionless, watches him keenly.*

Blackborough   I'm glad . . . heartily glad . . . that Mr O'Connell sees his way to keep silent. Frankly . . . not for your sake only. You're one of us already in a sense. Besides . . . these scandals weaken confidence in the whole governing class. . . .

Trebell   You're not answering my question.

Blackborough   No . . . it's for Horsham to answer . . . not for me.

Farrant   What question?

Blackborough   Why, my good Farrant . . . it's pretty plain, I take it, that however considerate Mr O'Connell here may be, this thing will be gossiped around . . . garbled, what's more . . . in the clubs and the Lobbies . . . among all the people that count . . . and want to count . . . and have it thought they count. No such thing as a secret nowadays! That's what's in your mind, isn't it, Trebell? Can you still carry through a Bill of this sort in an atmosphere of that sort? It's a question, no doubt.

Farrant *takes up the cudgels.*

Farrant   Why need there be gossip if we keep our mouths shut?

Blackborough   The tighter we shut 'em the more there'll be.

Farrant   Then we must find means to stop it.

Blackborough   If you make that discovery, Farrant, I'll see a statue's put up to you.

Farrant   Well . . . whatever the gossip . . . if we stand solid behind Trebell we can pull him through.

Blackborough   Oh . . . if we could postpone the Bill . . . !

Farrant   You know that's impossible.

Blackborough   Or if it were any sort of a Bill but a Church Bill . . . ! I may be wrong. I'd like to think so. I don't enjoy saying the unpleasant thing. But as well say it now as six weeks hence if it has to be said. However . . . it's for Horsham to decide . . . in the first place.

Is there a little sting in the tail of the sentence? Why should one suppose so? What he says sounds honest common sense. **Horsham** *is lulling.*

Horsham   I think we might perhaps wisely leave both well and ill alone just for this evening. And Mr O'Connell may be feeling that we have wandered from the point that concerns him.

From the beginning the situation has been on **Cantilupe**'s *nerves, none the less because he could speak calmly. But he now speaks his mind; distaste for the whole affair, and for his part in it, sounding in every word.*

Cantilupe   Cyril . . . you never should have brought me here. I hate to embarrass you further. I am thankful Mr O'Connell has decided as he has. But let it be clear, please, that I cannot now sit in a Cabinet with Mr Trebell.

No one shows surprise. **Trebell** *is, indeed, not surprised.* **O'Connell** *listens and looks, as a stranger in court may look on, tensely, at the climax of a trial. Only* **Farrant** *finds words.*

Farrant Well . . . I'm damned!

Cantilupe I'm sorry . . . and this may not seem the moment
to say it. But we've been at work upon the Bill together . . . for
three hours today we were at work upon it . . . we were to
meet again tomorrow. And I cannot . . . I cannot!

Horsham *is bitter-sweet.*

Horsham Thank you, my dear Charles . . . you do
embarrass me. The moment is ill-chosen . . . so far I agree
with you. I note your decision.

The position now gives **Blackborough** *the best of openings.*

Blackborough But, my dear Cantilupe, why rush to these
extremes?

Cantilupe I cannot discuss the matter.

Blackborough No, no . . . let's be helpful! I don't know
much about the Bill . . . I've not been consulted. Frankly . . .
what little I do know I don't like . . . and I wish we weren't
pledged to it. But now Trebell's out of the worst of his mess . .
. . let's do the best we can . . . though it mayn't be all we'd like
to do . . . for him . . . and the Bill . . . and the party . . . and
the country in general.

This all-embracing friendliness exasperates **Cantilupe** *beyond bearing.*

Cantilupe Convictions apart . . . how . . . how! . . . can I
sit in Cabinet with a man . . . and canvass my friends for his
Bill . . . for this Bill! . . . with such scandal for an unspoken end
and beginning of my every talk with them? It's impossible.

It is clearly time **O'Connell** *took his leave.*

O'Connell Will Dr Wedgecroft still be waiting for me? May
I wish you good evening, gentlemen? No, sir, you were right . .
. I can do nothing for you. And had revenge been what I
wanted . . . could I be leaving my interests in better hands?

He says this and passes by **Trebell** *towards the library door, at which*
Horsham *is standing.*

Horsham   Yes . . . he's here.

But at the door **O'Connell** *turns.*

O'Connell   Why don't you, though?

Trebell   Do what?

O'Connell   Speak the truth . . . if it's in you to? Outface the British lion in his smugness. If he didn't eat you . . . you could put your friends here in your pocket after, I think. Thank you, Mr Horsham.

So he departs; **Horsham**, *in courtesy, following him.*

Blackborough   Irish! Well . . . he would be.

Farrant   He'll hold his tongue. That's the great thing! Damn it, I believe he meant to all the time.

But **Trebell** *pays no attention; he has turned to* **Cantilupe**.

Trebell   Yes, Cantilupe . . . I'm an adulterer. So you'll have no more truck with me. Would our work be worthless? Is the thing in itself a deadly sin to you?

Cantilupe   Living in the world I live in, I have little right, perhaps, to call that a strange question. Yes . . . it is.

Trebell   And what's the atonement? Can you and your wise Church help me there?

Cantilupe   I fear not . . . when you ask unrepentant.

Trebell   Oh, I can repent . . . the thing done . . . and the folly of it. But the thing that I am . . . to repent that is to die.

Cantilupe   God help you, Trebell . . . God help you!

This talk between the two has been strangely like a talk between friends. **Horsham** *returns – returns to his troubles; but* **O'Connell** *at least he is rid of.*

Horsham   He's gone . . . they've both gone. I remember now why I interned him.

It is **Trebell**'s *turn now to say his say, and he says it without wasting time.*

Trebell   Horsham . . . I've not made you the usual gentlemanly offer to stand aside. This job means more to me. I wasn't sent into the world to make things easy for you. I warn you, Cantilupe . . . I can carry this Bill as it stands . . . and no one else will. You care for what's in it . . . and I care. You'll find no one else does. But if you do stick to me, Horsham . . . and Blackborough thinks this incongruous catastrophe and his kind help out of it will turn me into a biddable underling . . . he's mistaken.

Blackborough (*tartly*)   That's uncalled for.

Trebell   That mediaeval Irishman is right. There'll be poisonous gossip. Well . . . I'll tell the truth. I'll stand up in my place in the House and say: 'This I've done . . . this I am . . . this and no more I repent.' Will you back me after?

Farrant   By God . . . I believe we might!

Trebell   As a piece of policy I recommend it you. For if I win I'd carry the Bill for you without one bargain struck. If I go under . . . you'll be rid of a most uncomfortable colleague. I'll do it . . . I'm serious.

Blackborough   My dear fellow!

Horsham   Public life is not to be lived nowadays, I fear, on such heroic heights.

Trebell   Would that count for atonement, Cantilupe . . . would you stand by me then? Yes, indeed . . . we might put Worldly Wiseman and Facing-both-ways in our pockets afterwards. Well, Horsham . . . it's up to you. But make up your mind as quick as you can, please. You must, though, mustn't you? The job won't wait.

And he leaves them.

Blackborough   Half off his head!

Farrant   Do you wonder?

Blackborough   I met him on the doorstep. I thought
Wedgecroft would get him away.

Farrant   He nearly throttled m e !

Horsham's *thoughts are already a little removed.*

Horsham   I'm afraid, you know, that I always found her a
detestable little woman.

Farrant (*sturdily*)   I liked her. (*Then, candidly.*) My wife never
liked her.

Horsham   A harlot at heart! How much better then . . . for
all concerned . . . just to be a harlot.

Farrant   Well, whatever she was . . . and she's dead . . . and
I disagree with you . . . if he gets through tomorrow, you're
not going back on him, I trust. For that'd be damnable.

He has shot an angry glance at **Blackborough.**

Blackborough   I haven't suggested you should go back on
him . . . farther than you need go. Find him some other job.

Farrant   He won't take another job.

Blackborough   Oh . . . if he's going to be pig-headed!

Cantilupe   Cyril, if you think Trebell can take the Bill
through . . . you can do well enough without me. And I can do
as much for it from the back benches . . . and more, I daresay,
for the things in it that I've at heart.

Blackborough   Yes . . . I don't doubt you can.

He lets this out with such a bang that **Cantilupe** *turns to him, half
surprised, half angry.*

Cantilupe   What are you insinuating, may I ask?

Blackborough *now asserts himself.*

Blackborough   Horsham . . . when you do form your
Cabinet you'll ask whom you choose to join it. By summoning
us three, though, and Brampton . . . how is Brampton, by the
way?

Farrant   Better.

Blackborough   I'm glad . . . to this rescue party, you imply, I may take it, that you count on us?

Horsham   Quite.

Blackborough   Very good. We're pledged to a Church Bill of some sort. I wish we weren't . . .

Cantilupe   So you've told us . . . and we didn't need telling.

Horsham *grows the more pacific as* **Farrant** *grows angrier and* **Cantilupe** *snappier in his nervous distress.* **Blackborough,** *however, has no intention of losing his temper.*

Blackborough   My dear fellow . . . what good can it do us? At the best it's bound to be one of those damned cross-fire measures . . . with men opposite supporting you and your own side attacking you . . . disastrous to party discipline. You and Trebell have been cooking it up together . . .

Cantilupe   The Bill is his.

Blackborough   Brampton besides.

Horsham   He has seen the figures.

Blackborough   A most efficient little cabal.

Cantilupe   I object to that term.

Blackborough (*with perfect good humour*)   I withdraw it. And Trebell still talks of pushing the thing through the Cabinet . . . *sic volo, sic jubeo.* Plump and plain, I'd better tell you there may be things in it that won't at all suit me.

Cantilupe   For instance?

Blackborough   Well . . . as you've not done me the honour to consult me, I can't be very precise.

Horsham   I didn't know you were so interested in Church questions, Blackborough.

Blackborough   I'm not . . . nor in any political question till it has to be answered. But these rumours of Utopian educational schemes . . . seminaries for teachers . . . countryside universities! This isn't a time to be throwing the country's money about.

Cantilupe   It is the Church's money. Do you want to relieve the rates with it?

Blackborough   We might do worse mischief. Seriously, Cantilupe . . . you stand for the Church, twopence coloured. I stand for it, penny plain. Mine, that's to say, is the traditional British common-sense view of religion. Well, now . . . if you're going to leave us in the lurch with this Bill on our backs . . . not to mention Trebell, if Horsham thinks he can stick to him . . . I think we ought to have a pledge from you that you and your friends won't make trouble.

Cantilupe   Why should we?

Blackborough   Because you'll be free from responsibility and you'll want to get all you can. And what one's friends lose one's enemies gain. That's an axiom in politics.

Cantilupe (*hotly*)   I wish to get nothing for my friends that is inconsistent with justice and righteousness.

Blackborough   Quite so! So we all say!

Cantilupe   As long as this settlement . . . which the Bill provides for . . . as Trebell has drafted it and as Horsham has approved it . . . as long as that stands in its integrity . . . I shall support it.

Blackborough *casts his eyes towards the heaven which in its inscrutable wisdom has made such men as* **Cantilupe**. *But he treats him with masterly – if slightly masterful – patience.*

Blackborough   I'm sorry . . . I'm not making myself plain. I admit no settlement. If you're keen on parts of the Bill . . . stay in the Government and fight for them . . . and I'll fight you fair. If Horsham does drop Trebell I suppose you will stay. Need you insist on his being dropped altogether? Why not wait and see if scandal does spread? We shall soon know. Oh . . . if

mine were a foxy mind . . . I'd not be sorry, you'd think, to see
a Bill I dislike made a hash of by a man that . . . ! After all . . .
from the party point of view . . . he's an outsider. What has
Brampton to say, by the way?

Farrant   About all this? Oh, it was meat and drink to him.
He kept me an hour this afternoon telling me scandals of every
premier he'd served under. Not of you, Horsham.

Horsham   Whatever he may now know of me he can be
trusted to invent.

Blackborough   But about the Bill . . . has Trebell been
seeing him?

Farrant   Once or twice. He thinks the finance will be fun
because the Treasury will kick at it. But the fact is he's had a
grudge against Theobald Rogers there ever since his last
budget . . . and he wants to pay him out. If Trebell doesn't
come in, Brampton won't.

Blackborough   Really?

Farrant   Brampton thinks a lot of him.

If **Farrant** *had not been dead tired, he'd never have done it. As it is,
he stays innocent of what he has done.* **Horsham** *sees, but give hardly
a sign of seeing. What is the use?* **Blackborough**'s *speech is now
measured, his tone judicious.*

Blackborough   Brampton would be a loss. His mind's not
what it was . . . but he cuts a figure still. Well . . . there's
nothing more to say, for the moment, is there? Good-night.

He has, indeed, no more to say.

Farrant   But what is settled . . . about Trebell?

Cantilupe   Cyril . . . I wish to do whatever is best. But
consider my position.

Farrant   And consider our position if we drop Trebell and
he rounds on us. We shan't have fifty majority. And for this
sort of Bill there's bound to be cross-voting.

Blackborough   Then it won't be my sort of Bill. Our business is to compose our differences and bring in a Conservative Bill that a Conservative majority can vote for.

Cantilupe   That will be a worthless Bill.

Farrant   But we've laid down the principles of the thing and they've been approved of by the press and the public . . .

Blackborough   My good Farrant . . . don't talk like a patent medicine advertisement. Praise from the press in a chorus . . . they abuse you the worse later on . . . when they want something fresh to say. The public . . . can't hold an idea in its head as long as my dogs can.

Farrant   Trebell can knock now any Church Bill but his own to pieces in Committee. He could turn us out on it . . . and I shouldn't blame him.

Blackborough   No . . . it's the sort of thanks one gets for saving a man from gaol . . . yes, from gaol very likely. But I don't think so. Even he'd not have the hardihood to talk Christian statesmanship with the dirt of this scandal still spattered over him. Not that we should spread it abroad, of course, unless . . . ! No . . . I should always be against such meanness. But I shouldn't . . . in that case . . . feel called upon to contradict it. Horsham . . . you've been kindness itself to him. If you want to be kinder yet . . . in my opinion . . . you'll drop him and let him go back to the Bar for a bit . . . he must have been making his pile there. Or put him on the Bench. You've a reputation as a cynic. The Divorce Court ought to be vacant soon. Seriously . . . ! But you don't need my advice. Still . . . you'd rather I made my position clear.

He has made himself, his position, and his intentions crystal clear to **Horsham**, *who replies very drily . . .*

Horsham   Much.

Blackborough   Good-night.

Horsham   Thank you for coming.

Blackborough   Can I drop you, Farrant?

Farrant   No, I'll walk . . . thanks. (*The gratitude more an effort than an afterthought*).

Blackborough   Right! Don't come down.

He departs. He has done a good evening's work and knows it. They detest him.

Farrant   And what sort of a very private life has he led, I wonder.

Horsham   I should suppose that his relations with the gentler sex have always been businesslike . . . most businesslike. The social scandals of the Industrial North do not, however, penetrate to our sophisticated world . . . a fact, of which, we must hope, no undue advantage is taken.

Horsham *can always salve his troubles with a little acrid humour. Lucky man!*

Farrant   Well . . . what is settled? It's very late.

Horsham   What's settled? . . . Since you so recklessly keep asking! Why . . . that I drop Trebell.

Farrant – *bless him!* – *is surprised.*

Farrant   D'you mean it?

Horsham   My dear George . . . if, after listening to Blackborough, you imagine he now means to let me form a Cabinet with Trebell in it . . . I must admire your innocence.

Farrant   But . . . good God! . . . is one to be bullied by Blackborough? Leave h i m out, then.

Horsham   I should love to . . . and his friends and relations besides.

Farrant   No . . . you can't. Get him in, then, with Trebell . . . and assert yourself.

Horsham   No leader who needs to do that, George, must ever dare to.

Farrant   Oh, don't be paradoxical . . . I'm tired. I don't see, though . . . if O'Connell stands pat . . . what more Blackborough can do now than he always could have done.

Horsham   Don't you? Brampton, who despises him . . . Charles here, with some prestige in Church matters . . . and Trebell, till this happened . . . were a pretty strong combination. He'd have had to knuckle under to it. Break it up . . . and there's his chance . . . as he saw.

Cantilupe   But isn't this the heart-breaking thing in politics? Some great chance . . . if every circumstance will conspire in its favour. One slip . . . and it's against it they're conspiring.

Horsham   I am glad you appreciate that, Charles.

Horsham *has gone to a writing-table and is beginning a letter.*
Cantilupe *begins across the room rather pathetically.*

Cantilupe   My saying I'd stand out made the mischief, d'you mean?

Farrant *rounds on him quite brutally.*

Farrant   Well, what else? Serve you damn well right, Charles, if your Bill is wrecked.

Cantilupe   But Blackborough saw the situation sooner than I did.

Horsham   Still . . . never play your opponent's game for him. Your temperament, Charles, leads you to embrace misfortunes.

Farrant *thinks a little blame may as well be put on* **Horsham**.

Farrant   Why did you bring him here tonight anyhow?

Horsham   Oh . . . he's as touchy as a beauty losing her looks. If I'd left him out . . . ! No, no . . . no, no, no! Flattering him into playing the magnanimous . . . that was the only chance.

Cantilupe   He's after the Exchequer himself, I suppose.

Horsham   Yes . . . and he'll get it now . . . I've no one else.
When you let out we'd lose Brampton, George, he launched
his ultimatum . . . did you notice? No . . . you didn't.

Farrant   But . . . good God! . . . why didn't you stop me?

Poor **Farrant**; *the tables are turned on him!*

Horsham   I'd as soon know how I stand tonight as know it
a week hence . . . and sooner. What's Trebell's number in
Berkeley Street?

Farrant   Forty-seven.

Then they both realise what the letter is. Veritably a funereal air falls.

Cantilupe   Are you writing to tell him now?

Horsham   Yes.

Farrant   I say! . . . Can't you wait a bit? Something may
happen.

Horsham   No.

Farrant   I hate this.

They feel guilty and look it. **Horsham** *addresses his envelope.*

Cantilupe   But, Cyril . . . who's to take the Bill through?

Horsham   I don't know yet. I can't . . . there's the FO
complication. I rather advise you to stand clear and screw out
of us any scraps of the old scheme that you'd really set your
heart on. I shall find somebody.

He says it quite cheerfully. He always has found somebody.

Farrant   I don't care so much about the Bill . . . but I do bar
Trebell's being dished . . . just when we'd got him clear from
the real mess too. What fools it leaves us looking! Surely,
Horsham, with your authority . . .

Horsham *has finished his letter and addressed and closed it.*

Horsham   You take, I think, a romantic view of my office, and, consequently . . . though I don't complain . . . an unromantic one of me. What authority will make men abler . . . or more honest . . . or less selfish than they are? I have to match you all with − and against − each other, so that from the heat of your differences a little power to do something may, if possible, result. The art of the thing lies in having such a quick sense of what won't work that before we've all quarrelled irretrievably I have set you to something else that will. Shall I post this . . . or had one of you better see that he gets it tonight?

Farrant   I won't face him.

Horsham   Dear Uncle Mark started me as his secretary at twenty-three . . . and he taught me to nourish no political illusions. Yet at sixty-five I am tempted to try this rather imaginative stroke . . . and I fail. I'm not surprised. But the calculation was such a nice one . . . such a combining of incompatibles! What a triumph − and how amusing − to have brought it off! Would you post this, then, in the corner pillar-box as you pass?

He has found a stamp in his pocket-book and has carefully stuck it on. But these reflections are of small comfort to **Farrant**, *who is feeling savage.*

Farrant   I just hope Trebell will give us hell next session . . . that's all.

Cantilupe   What will happen to him, I wonder, Cyril?

Horsham   Hard to say. Most men's careers work to a climax . . . and if they miss their moment the best of them may sink back to nonentity. A pity in this case . . . a pity. By the bye, Charles, there was something else I wanted a word with you about. The Giorgione portrait. Your mother mustn't sell it.

They have found their way to the door. **Farrant**, *indeed, is already on his way downstairs. But the two cousins pause in the doorway.*

Cantilupe   But she needs the money.

Horsham   But it's the copy, I do assure you. It's the original that's at Holcroft. My father told me the whole story. Fotheringham got it out of Great-aunt Jane. He was cracked about pictures after he was sixty. She'd been his mistress, undoubtedly . . . and their later relations were unspeakable. All sorts of references to them had to be cut out of Creevey and . . . what's that other book?

Cantilupe   But Mother must pay her income tax.

Horsham   Well . . . if she tries to sell that picture all these old stories will be raked up. It will be most unpleasant for her . . .

They go out together talking

Act Four

Trebell's room in the evening looks as you would expect it to look, except that, this evening, the curtains of the window are drawn back, and we are conscious of the strange London darkness, which is never dark, outside. **Trebell** *and* **Wedgecroft** *come up the stairs talking.* **Wedgecroft** *carries his hat and wears his overcoat.*

Wedgecroft   Yes . . . when I saw the light I whistled the tune without a thought . . . and down you came!

Trebell   I was thinking . . . at the moment . . . of my old room in Gower Street.

He puts a period to this preface by whistling the signal tune — all ardent Wagnerians used it in the eighteen-nineties — the Siegfried sword motif. Then **Wedgecroft** *begins.*

Wedgecroft   Well . . . we're safe, I'm sure. O'Connell won't go back on you.

Trebell   He's not committed to flat perjury, I hope. Nor you?

Wedgecroft   Oh . . . I rank as an expert witness.

Trebell   Has the thing hit him very hard?

Wedgecroft   He's at odds with the world.

Trebell   He can slip back to his thirteenth century . . . after tomorrow. Well, what more can you do for me, Gilbert? I've been a lot of trouble to you, I'm afraid.

For **Wedgecroft** *is regarding him with a quizzical and not unanxious eye, in which friendly and professional concern are mixed.* **Trebell's** *voice has, indeed, an oddly hollow ring, and he walks with a curious lightness, as a man may feel himself walking in a dream.*

Wedgecroft   I'd like you to get some sleep tonight. When was your last good night's sleep?

Trebell   I haven't slept for a night or so.

Wedgecroft   I see. You'll swallow two of these when you go to bed . . .

He has fetched a little bottle out of his pocket, taken an envelope from the writing-table and is shaking some pellets into it.

Trebell   No, no. They upset my inside . . . and my dignity.

Wedgecroft   . . . and two more an hour later if need be.

Trebell   Why not acid drops? Just as effective! I won't go to bed . . . that's the simplest plan.

Wedgecroft   Confound you! . . . I'm thinking of your job, not of you. You must keep fit for it.

Trebell   I told her that.

The casual inconsequence of this is jarring. But **Wedgecroft** *holds his professional course.*

Wedgecroft   It has been a bad business. But drop the curtain of one good night's sleep on it . . . and I'll soon have you back to normal. By the way . . . how much . . . now . . . is Frances to know?

Trebell   How much does she know? She'd hold her tongue to me . . . and expect me to hold mine to her. But she may have to be told now. Horsham may be throwing me over, after all.

This, though, does knock **Wedgecroft** *off his balance.*

Wedgecroft   No!

Trebell   Yes.

Wedgecroft   In Heaven's name . . . why?

Trebell   It must be so vexing for you, Gilbert, to pull a patient through . . . and have him run over in the street a week after. And I'm told that then his executors always grumble when there's your bill to pay.

Wedgecroft   Why the devil didn't I let you go to O'Connell when you wanted to? They need never have known.

Trebell   True! I've been thinking of that. But they may not throw me over. I left them in conclave. So don't hint anything to Frances. She has just come in . . . I heard the car. Farrant will stroll round to tell me, I daresay. The window's for his benefit.

Wedgecroft   If they throw you over now . . . the next one that calls me in . . . I'll poison him.

Trebell   That's the spirit! But I rather wish I'd not given my virgin heart to a Bill of disestablishing the Church of England. Reckless of me!

Frances *comes upstairs hurriedly, a little breathless, disturbed.*

Frances Trebell   Henry! Oh, Gilbert . . . I'm so glad you're here.

Trebell   *Meistersingers* over early?

Frances Trebell   It's past twelve.

Trebell   I said early.

Frances Trebell   I'm terribly upset. I heard as I was coming out in the crowd . . . Amy O'Connell's dead.

The two men keep their composure, but the talk takes on a certain restraint.

Trebell   Gilbert has been telling me.

Frances Trebell   I knew she was ill. You weren't attending her?

Wedgecroft   Yes.

Frances Trebell   But there's to be an inquest.

Wedgecroft   Tomorrow.

Frances Trebell   What's been wrong? Mustn't I ask?

Trebell   I'll tell you. Gilbert's tired. He has done a day's work . . . and a bit.

Wedgecroft   Good-night, then. Take that stuff. I'll be round about nine-thirty . . . but if I hear you snoring I'll be the better pleased.

Frances Trebell   Are you ill, Henry? Hasn't he been sleeping?

Wedgecroft   He's not ill. A nice little illness now and then . . . a little lowering of the physical pride . . . might be very good for him. Bless you both.

Frances Trebell   Bless you, dear Gilbert.

Trebell   Pull the door to, hard, would you? The lock's loose or something.

Wedgecroft *leaves them together.*

Frances Trebell   What about Amy?

Trebell   An unwelcome baby was on the way. She went to some quack . . . and Gilbert couldn't save her.

Frances Trebell   Yes . . . that's the gossip. Terrible! Doubly terrible! The little fool! The little runaway!

One discovers **Frances** *has a taste of her brother's ruthlessness. His response is somewhat acid.*

Trebell   The celibate's comment.

She has had, one must remember, half an hour in which to grieve for Amy's death; so her lively good sense is already in the ascendant.

Frances Trebell   No . . . come now! One may choose one's lot in life . . . but having chosen it . . . !

Trebell   True. I didn't mean to gibe.

Frances Trebell   That wasn't all the trouble, though . . . surely?

Trebell   I daresay not.

Frances Trebell   Some affair she'd been having . . . ?

Trebell   I daresay.

Frances Trebell   Even so . . . couldn't she have found someone with common sense to turn to . . . some woman? Heavens . . . I didn't like her much . . . but I'd have done what I could. No . . . there it was! She was pretty and popular . . . she could make a party go . . . and men flirted with her. But when it came to this . . . she knew none of us liked her much. Oh . . . death leave things so frustrated, doesn't it? I'd meant to go round there this morning. I think she did like me a little. Egoist! Another debt, then, I'll never pay.

Trebell   I shouldn't worry about that. Our likes and dislikes go the round . . . in various disguises. The sum of the getting and giving works out pretty fairly.

This is sufficiently cryptic for **Frances** *to ask him – though without too much intention . . .*

Frances Trebell   Is this all you know?

Trebell   It's all I can tell you for the moment.

They have a habit, these two, of saying what they mean to each other and accepting the thing said. It has been a businesslike and not such a bad relationship.

Frances Trebell   Then I'll go to bed. Not that I'll sleep.

Trebell   Try Gilbert's physic.

Frances Trebell   Poor Amy! Poor little fool!

Trebell   Her epitaph.

Frances Trebell   Fear of life . . . the beginning of all evil.

Trebell   Is it?

Frances Trebell   I've come to think so.

Trebell   I've wondered lately whether you did right to give up your work to turn housekeeper for me.

Frances Trebell   It's a little late to be wondering that.

Trebell   You were a pretty good teacher . . . and that's moral motherhood of a sort. Your young women here were fond of you. Could you go back to it?

Frances Trebell   I wasn't very fond of them, I fear. Reason enough for giving up. I can spare you the self-sacrificing sister. No . . . I couldn't go back.

Trebell   This need to care for people, Frankie, is the devil and all.

Frances Trebell   And when did it begin to trouble you? And what makes you call me by my nursery name for the first time in thirty years?

Trebell   I don't know. But I should have sent you packing perhaps. Why . . . we've never even had a quarrel.

To which touch of wan humour she responds.

Frances Trebell   All the domestic joys missed. Never mind. You've been a credit to me. And time begins to slip by for us pretty quickly now, doesn't it? Good-night. Shall I give you these?

'These' are **Wedgecroft**'s *soporifics. But* **Trebell**'s *thoughts are far from such matters.*

Trebell   No . . . no, thank you.

She goes towards him, as if – though not intrusively – she would like to get a little nearer to him, in another sense, if she could.

Frances Trebell   There's nothing troubling you . . . that you'd like to tell me?

Trebell   No.

Nothing harsh about it; again, he just means what he says. But now, for a wonder, she does not leave it at that.

Frances Trebell   Has it been my fault you've never confided in me? You hate women . . . I've heard you say . . . when you can't altogether despise them. Yet I'm not so very womanly . . . in the worst sense . . . am I? If I thought you could ever come

to be unhappy . . . as other people are . . . it would make me
unhappy to be such a stranger to you.

Trebell   If I ever come to be . . . waste no time on me. The
egoist gone soft . . . I know nothing more contemptible.

Frances Trebell   No . . . you see other men so starkly as
they are . . . you're not built to be disillusioned about yourself.
And you've never had a failure . . . never even been crossed in
love . . .

Trebell   Never come within reach of the good woman's
gospel of salvation. And I think, thank you, I'll keep out of it to
the end. Go to bed . . . go to bed. I've to sit up for a bit yet . . .
I'm expecting a message.

Frances Trebell   At this hour? And I don't even ask what
about . . . though that would be human . . . even womanly!
Very well. Don't work, though . . . or sit and think. You're
tired. I'll choose you a book.

Trebell   My mind was never clearer.

Frances Trebell   The rest of you is the more tired. Mark
Twain?

As she moves to the bookcase those familiar red volumes face her.

Trebell   Good . . . not a woman's choice, either. *Huck Finn*,
please. Mark was a sound fellow. He had comic courage. A gift.
I'd choose it, I think, before any. Man's last weapon against
the gods. When he's at his puniest . . . he can still laugh them
into littleness . . . and come to his own standing again. Thank
you. I'll give Mark his chance . . . to stop me thinking . . . if he
can.

Frances Trebell   But I can't help?

Trebell   No.

Frances Trebell   Very well.

*Still his rejection of her is not harsh, nor purposefully cold. But the blank
chill of it seems to rouse some inward anger in her now, as if her care for*

him must somehow struggle for its life. But the anger, too, stays dumb, and she turns away and leaves him.

Early the next morning she finds him there. He has not moved, to all appearances. The fire is out, the lights are out; through the window, with its drawn-back curtains, can be seen London's grey autumn sky. **Frances** *has been disturbed in her dressing and has thrown a wrap about her to come down. The night has broken her composure, but it has set his hard.*

Frances Trebell   Henry!

Trebell   Yes?

Frances Trebell   Bertha says you've not been to bed all night.

Trebell   She's quite right. She came in to do the room. I fear I startled her.

Frances Trebell   I waited to hear you come up. I came down once to listen. Then I fell asleep. Did you fall asleep down here?

Trebell   No . . . I've not been to sleep.

Frances Trebell   I must know what's wrong. What was the message? What has happened?

Trebell   The message didn't come. There might be a letter. Are they here yet?

Frances Trebell   Yes . . . I don't know . . . Yours are put in Walter's room.

Trebell   I'll see.

He goes across to the little room and returns with a pile of twenty letters, it may be. He finds her, head bowed, face hidden, and she does not look up. As he sees her thus, suddenly forty years fall away; for so he has seen her time and again, in their rather shabby nursery schoolroom, childishly grieving. And the difference is not so great.

Trebell   My dear . . . don't cry. You've had a bad night too . . . and what was the use of that?

Frances Trebell   I'm not crying. I never cry.

Trebell   What then?

Frances Trebell   I think I was trying to pray.

Trebell   Help me to look through these. The thing may be settled . . . past praying for.

He gives her a half of the letters and they begin to open them.

Frances Trebell   But I'm still angry, I'm afraid. When you said I couldn't help you . . . though God knows I knew it! . . . it made me angry to have you say it. But if I'd not been angry it would have hurt too badly. You may as well tell me the facts now about Amy O'Connell.

Mechanically, as she asks him, she is opening and glancing at the letters, putting them in an orderly pile, tearing the envelopes. He, as he answers her, is doing the same.

Trebell   Yes . . . it was my child.

Frances Trebell   I'm a blind fool, I suppose. I never guessed you were in love with her.

Trebell   I wasn't.

Frances Trebell   She with you, then.

Trebell   It didn't last long. The little trull!

The thing is wrung from him. It releases her anger.

Frances Trebell   Henry . . . how can you be so vile as to say that of her . . . now?

Trebell   It's the truth.

Frances Trebell   Whatever she was, you were. And she has paid.

Trebell   I've to pay. Whatever she'd done but this . . . I'd have faced it. Let's go through these letters.

Her anger is exhausted. The letter-opening has come to a standstill. Mechanically they start again.

Frances Trebell   If you'd loved her . . . only a little . . . s h e might have found courage to face it.

At this he turns to her in sudden poignant uncertainty.

Trebell   D'you think so?

She is honest.

Frances Trebell   No. We are what we are, I suppose.

Trebell   Then don't let us cant.

Frances Trebell   Will you dine with the Anglican League . . . and speak?

Trebell   Put it over there . . . Walter can answer it.

The letter reminds her . . .

Frances Trebell   But what's to happen? Are people to know?

Trebell   I've been got off that much.

Frances Trebell   This is marked 'Private'.

Trebell   Begging letter probably!

Frances Trebell   Oh . . . I know what she was. But you who've despised the best of us . . . and the best in us . . . you to be caught in the trap the cheapest women can spread!

Frances *does not, perhaps, quite comprehend the masculine nature.* **Trebell** *(at this moment even) is a little short with her.*

Trebell   The best or the worst of you, my dear . . . if you'll all but go your own way and make it a straight way . . . we know where we are with you then.

Frances Trebell   This is from Horsham . . . he always initials his envelopes, doesn't he?

He asks for the letter (by a gesture) precisely, and yet, it would seem, indifferently. But this is not indifference; it is something far harder to survive, detachment. **Trebell** *is now taking a cool but genuine interest — in someone else's affairs.*

Frances Trebell   Don't let us be harsh with each other . . . now. That's Cousin Robert's hand.

She pushes him over another letter. He has glanced through **Horsham**'s *note, which* **Farrant** *had put in the pillar-box the night before.*

Trebell   Thank you. Horsham will have no use for me in his Government.

Frances Trebell   Oh! Does that follow?

Frances *is blank at the news. Having finished* **Horsham**'s *letter, he begins Cousin Robert's.*

Trebell   Well . . . it has. Robert says it seems a long time since they had the pleasure of seeing me at Winfield . . . but that now I'm a greater man than ever I must of course be very busy. But he has been busy too . . . over a bazaar to raise money for his boys' club. And they've re-papered the rectory throughout . . . except the servants' rooms, which were done six years ago . . . and that has been an upset. And Mary sends you her love and hopes you've had no return of your rheumatism. And he wonders, if he could find time to run up to town, whether I wouldn't like an afternoon's talk with him upon my Disestablishment schemes. For, after all, his practical experience of the work of a country parish . . .

Slowly — for she is tired and her emotions have been stunned — the full scope of the catastrophe has opened out to **Frances**. *And his detachment from it is the more dreadful to her.*

Frances Trebell   Don't, Henry . . . don't! I can't bear it.

Trebell   But he's quite right. I ought to have had a talk with him. And he remains my affectionate cousin. He has the neatest little signature.

A silence.

Frances Trebell   Horsham's quite definite?

Trebell   He is kind enough to be.

Frances Trebell   Was it inevitable? Why . . . if there's to be no scandal?

Trebell   A scandal half stifled is worse than a scandal. One is at everybody's mercy. That's their excuse . . . but it isn't their reason for getting rid of me. No . . . I knew! I was trying them pretty high. Take the hard path and you can't afford to slip . . . the easier world is in a natural conspiracy against you.

Frances Trebell   But Horsham believed in you . . . and your plan.

Trebell   Very nearly. But he'd have had a horrid time with me.

Frances Trebell   It'll tumble to pieces without you.

Trebell   They'll patch up something . . . they'll muddle something through.

Frances Trebell   The best of it did seem too good to be true.

Trebell   If I were God that's the one blasphemy I'd not forgive.

From the vengeful force of this you'd say there was hope in the man still. And – though she may not know it is this – it inspires her with a broken sort of hope.

Frances Trebell   Well, my dear . . . what now? All this will lie heavy on you for a little. But I see fifty futures for you still.

Trebell *might almost be amused; it is so easy to be hopeful for others.*

Trebell   Do you?

Frances Trebell   You're a free lance again. You made your name fighting the lot of them.

But somehow it doesn't sound very hopeful.

Trebell   We don't travel the same road twice . . . except as ghosts. Oh . . . I could still make a show of success. Have my revenge on them too! A barren business. No. I'm done. I've come to the end. Walter will finish the letters.

He says it all so simply that it might mean little – or much.

Frances Trebell To the end?

Trebell As far as I can see.

And the careless simplicity of that is suspicious.

Frances Trebell That can't mean with you . . . what one
might fear it to mean. Besides . . . if it did, you wouldn't be
telling me, would you? But I know the feeling. It has deadened
us all at some time. It's a sign, though, that the worst's over.

He turns to her with a curious air of kindly, cold reproval.

Trebell If I'm to confide in you . . . for once! . . . better
believe I mean what I say.

Frances Trebell But this one piece of work . . . had it come
to mean everything to you?

Trebell More.

Frances Trebell More?

Trebell Yes. I'd never, so to speak, given myself away
before. It's a dreadful joy to do that . . . to become part of a
purpose bigger than your own. Another strength is added to
your own . . . it's a mystery. But it follows, you see, that having
lost myself in the thing . . . the loss of it leaves me a dead man.

*There is the sort of logic about this that speaks of the toppling mind. She
eyes him rather fearfully, but her voice is calm, is comforting.*

Frances Trebell Yes . . . I understand. But these are only
words.

Trebell D'you think so? Death is a fact to be faced. And
what is it that dies? One may be dead for years . . . and who'll
notice . . . if one keeps up appearances? It's not good manners
to notice. But why cumber the ground? I once heard four
doctors . . . Gilbert among them . . . disputing the moment,
the exact moment, when they'd a right to say: This is death.
I thought the corpse ought to know. And after some days . . .
and nights . . . of consideration, I'm of the opinion that in all
that matters to me I'm a dead man.

Frances Trebell   You're a sick man. And suffering is so strange to you.

Trebell   I'm not suffering . . . far from it. While one suffers, one lives, I suppose.

Frances Trebell   Then there's a deeper hurt. Is it her death that's haunting you? But you didn't love her, you say.

He responds a little wearily: what have the dead to do with such mortal matters?

Trebell   Can't you forgive me that? You'd hardly have forgiven me if I had.

Frances Trebell   Oh . . . I can be callous about her . . . if it'll help. What was she but a bit of base pleasure to you? And not fit to be more! Let's forget her then.

Trebell   I keep thinking of the child.

Frances Trebell   Is t h a t the trouble?

Trebell   Why . . . has it no right to be?

This, oddly enough, is a new and unexpected light on the matter to **Frances**. *But, surely, there can be no incurable trouble here.*

Frances Trebell   My dear . . . it was dreadful . . . the thing she did . . . dreadfully wrong. But after all . . . babies enough don't get born. We must take a practical view of it.

A rueful little smile flickers across his face, and is gone.

Trebell   Women do . . . for they have to . . . who's to blame them? But men's travail is of the soul. And if this new power coming to birth in me has been killed now . . . as wantonly as she denied life to that child . . . I'd rather like to think that Fate could be so subtle in revenge.

Whatever answer can she make?

Frances Trebell   This isn't sane! It isn't sane!

Trebell By other measure than our thrifty sanity my life may well be of no more account than that balked scrap of being was.

If she can say nothing to combat these delusions — monstrous delusions! — she must do something at least. She has hold of his hand, she can grip his arm; and these are alive.

Frances Trebell I shan't leave you . . . till you've promised . . : to do nothing foolish.

This time he smiles irrefutably.

Trebell We can't sit here, you know, and hold hands for ever. And if I meant to add that death to the other . . . though I've not said I mean to, have I? . . . a jump from the window and a broken neck . . . or a broken promise . . . yes, even to you! . . . what could be simpler?

She does not loose him; she searches desperately for other help.

Frances Trebell Will you come away with me?

Trebell Where?

Frances Trebell I don't think it matters . . . as long as we cut free, for a little, from this tangle of failure. What's to stop us walking out the door and away . . . this very minute?

He is provokingly patient.

Trebell Nothing.

Frances Trebell Let's break prison, my dear . . . no matter how. D'you remember being taken from school that summer Mother was dying . . . and sent out all day . . . and we followed back each one of those streams in the hills there till we found out where it rose? Well, let's go gipsying now . . . we're not so dreadfully middle-aged. We could turn our backs to the sea, once we'd crossed it. We could walk up a real river now. That's the only right way to the mountains. We'd reach them by spring-time . . . when the passes are opening . . . and you see flowers in the snow. I did walk down into Carinthia once . . . one Easter . . . sleeping where I found myself when night

came . . . and the people were so simple and kind. Why stay in
a prison just because you've built it . . . when the whole world
belongs to you? We'll walk on and on . . . day after day . . .
and not talk much . . . and only be tired in body . . . till we feel
alive again . . . and in tune again . . . till the touch of common
things has healed us.

Trebell   And till we finish where we started. What a pity the
world's round! The most depressing discovery ever made.
Should we write a book too? You've the romantic touch. But
a tour of the Empire's my move, surely . . . by all the rules!

She has failed.

Frances Trebell   Very well. It should be some comfort,
I suppose, to find you can still mock at me.

Trebell   I'm sorry. But the fact is that, for a selfish man, I'm
not as much interested in myself as you might think. I'm done
for . . . I'm done with. I wish my job were done . . . but, really,
it would be pompous to complain. If I'd life in me . . . nothing
that has happened would matter a straw. I've none . . . so do
I matter? And I'm quite sane, I assure you. I've not been
sleeping, it's true. But I read *Huck Finn* for an hour and had a
good laugh. I was hungry . . . and I raided the larder for some
bread and cheese. I said I'd give one more sunrise its chance.
But my light's out.

What more can she say or do? She speaks calmly.

Frances Trebell   Very well. I won't vex you any more now,
as long as I know . . . don't promise; I don't want a promise . . .
that you'll do nothing foolish . . . or irretrievable. And we'll
have another talk in a week's time, shall we? After all . . .
what's a week . . . now the worst's over? And you'll sleep now.

Trebell   I'd be glad of some sleep.

She has freed him; and she stands by him, watchfully, would-be trustfully.

Frances Trebell   I love you . . . you're all I've ever loved.
Till you are yourself again . . . find a little life in that.

He does not answer. There is an empty moment.

Trebell   But now you must get dressed, mustn't you? And I need a shave . . . so don't lock up my razors.

She gives a wan little laugh.

Frances Trebell   I'd meant to.

Trebell   What's a week . . . as you say . . . or a year . . . or ten? Who'd bargain for a life on such terms . . . even if he could? Time's no measure, is it, of the things men have made honourable? And whatever our failings, Frankie, we've meant to live . . . you and I . . . in the large freedom of the mind. So let's be true to it. My faith . . . a man needs one when he faces the ignorance of death . . . is that Nature is spendthrift . . . yet the God to whose creating we travail may be infinitely economical and waste, perhaps, less of the wealth of us when we're dead than we waste in the faithlessness and slavery of our lives.

That much liveliness of thought in him seems to comfort her. And she is so ready to find comfort.

Frances Trebell   My dear! I've not been very sane myself, I think. But all's well now . . . all's going to be.

Trebell   That's a large order. Here's Bertha come to do the room.

Bertha *had appeared, somewhat doubtfully. But hearing this last she takes it she is to do the room at last.* **Bertha** *has the air of a housemaid many years settled in her place, whom town life has never despoiled of her country training. The tension of their talk together thus finally broken,* **Frances** *turns to go, in ease of mind now, giving a final look at her brother and saying . . .*

Frances Trebell   And we might break prison for a little . . . all the same.

When she has gone he begins to pick up the letters from the table, keeping them, as far as he can, in their tidied heaps.

Trebell   Give me those, will you? Then you can dust. Did you have a good holiday?

Bertha   Yes, sir . . . thank you, sir. And I hope you had the same.

To be sure; not three weeks ago he was in Italy!

Trebell   Yes, thank you, Bertha . . . so I did!

He carries the letters through to leave them on **Walter Kent**'s *table, and comes out again, closing the door behind him with a certain decision. Then he goes upstairs, leaving* **Bertha** *to do the room.*

An hour or so later (the room has been done) we find **Wedgecroft** *sitting at the big table writing a letter.* **Frances**, *fully dressed now, comes upstairs and stands beside him, waiting for him to finish before she speaks. But he does not keep her waiting so long. When she speaks there is death in her voice, as in her face – though not her own death.*

Wedgecroft   Yes?

Frances Trebell   Horsham's downstairs . . . and I can't see him . . . I can't! He has come to sympathise, I suppose. What are you writing?

Wedgecroft   Only a note to . . . to the police surgeon. All right . . . I'll see Horsham.

Frances Trebell   I've taken the revolver out of his hand. Was that wrong . . . shouldn't I have touched it?

Wedgecroft   No, of course not! You must stay out of the room. I ought to have locked the door.

Frances Trebell   I'm sorry. I couldn't bear, somehow, to see the revolver in his hand. I won't go back. He's not there in the room any more, is he? But the spirit must stay by the body for a little, you'd think. And his face is so eager still.

Wedgecroft   Hush . . . hush!

He puts out a soothing hand towards hers, and she pulls herself together again. **Lady Julia Farrant** *has come quietly into the room. She stands for a moment, sympathetically silent, till* **Frances**, *conscious of her, turns. Sympathy is unnerving; she droops into* **Lady Julia**'s *arms.*

Frances Trebell   Julia!

Lady Julia   Oh . . . dear friend . . . poor friend! I brought
Cyril Horsham. He felt he must come.

Wedgecroft   I'll see him.

*He speaks brusquely. His compassion is not at all of this kind. He has
finished his letter. He gets up and goes downstairs.* **Lady Julia** *makes*
Frances *sit down and sits down by her.*

Lady Julia   Don't try to talk. Walter has told me . . . just
what happened.

But **Frances** *is herself again.*

Frances Trebell   I don't mind talking. I was in my
bedroom when I heard the shot. We'd been sitting here
together not ten minutes before.

Lady Julia   But why . . . oh, why? Not because he's lost this
chance of office? That wasn't like him. Oh . . . I don't want
Cyril Horsham to think that! And even if the scandal had
broken . . . nowadays everything's forgotten so soon. No one
dreamed her death would upset him so.

*Frances turns an inquiring gaze on her friend, who now, indeed, seems
more distracted – certainly more unguarded – than she.*

Frances Trebell   Did you know . . . about Amy?

Lady Julia   No one k n e w, of course . . . and it couldn't
have lasted any time. But she always had to show off her
conquests. People joked about it for a week or two.

Frances Trebell   I never knew. Why didn't you tell me?
I might have saved her.

Lady Julia   My dear . . . how could I? Besides, you never
wanted to know . . . about that sort of thing.

Frances sits silent for a moment. Then she looks at **Lady Julia**
*again; but no longer questioningly, rather as if all questions were now
answered.*

Frances Trebell   We should never have had anything to
do with you, Julia . . . no, not with any of you . . . he or I. We
weren't your sort, I'm afraid. Will you go away now, please?

No trace of anger in her voice. But **Lady Julia** *is amazed, hurt,
wounded and bereft of words.*

Lady Julia   Frances . . . dear Frances!

Frances Trebell   Oh . . . I'm sure you're very fond of me.
You're not heartless . . . you and the rest of you . . . nor
hypocrites . . . nor even so selfish as you might be. For you've
just got to be greedy, haven't you, of the things you need from
the people who can help keep you where you are? And you
were making good use of him. You've always been kind to me,
Julia . . . and I'm fond of you, too. I never quite lost my head,
did I, in your flattering world? Nor he! We both knew the
worth of it, I think . . . and our worth to you. But for all that,
I suppose we weren't wise enough at heart in its ways. And now
he's dead in the toils of them. Yes . . . you're sorry, I'm sure . . .
and you're still kind. But he was half my life to me . . . and more.
So now will you let us be strangers again for a little, please?

Lady Julia*, recovered, makes with gentleness, with dignity, with true
kindliness and affection, what is surely the right answer.*

Lady Julia   Dear Frances . . . there's nothing you mayn't say
to me . . . and in anger . . . if that eases the hurt. Only don't
think that things said so are true . . . for then to have said them
makes the hurt worse later on.

As if the hurt mattered! As if (*thinks* **Frances**) *anything they could feel
or say or do would bring him back! But all she says is . . .*

Frances Trebell   I am not angry.

Walter Kent*, head dropped, fists clenched, comes upstairs and turns
into his own room.* **Wedgecroft** *follows him and comes in to fetch the
letter he wrote.*

Wedgecroft   Horsham is just going. He asked me to tell you
he was sure he could keep the worst out of the papers. He

thought you'd be staying with Frances, Lady Julia. Can he have your car?

There is something in all this, and in his tone, which does not, somehow, support **Horsham**'s *reputation for sympathy – of which* **Lady Julia** *is very tender.*

Lady Julia   But he's dreadfully upset, isn't he? Have you ever seen him so upset?

Wedgecroft   Never.

Dear **Wedgecroft** *is really most uncompromising. She gets up to go.*

Lady Julia   Send for me soon, Frances dear. Tell Walter to. You'll have him here to help, won't you? He's heart-broken.

Frances Trebell   Yes. Thank you, Julia. You're very kind.

As it happens she has said it quite mechanically; her thoughts are in that room upstairs. But poor **Lady Julia** *is flooded by self-consciousness and says in deprecating protest . . .*

Lady Julia   No . . . not just kind! Do believe that . . . do try to believe that of me, Frances . . . please!

Frances Trebell   Yes, yes . . . I'll believe it.

If she'll only go! She goes; a little hurt, but as sympathetic as when she came. **Wedgecroft**'s *brusqueness is a comforting change.*

Wedgecroft   Don't let anyone else fuss you. I'll come back and see to things. But I have to go now . . . for an hour.

Frances Trebell   To the other inquest.

Wedgecroft (*unwillingly*)   Yes.

Frances Trebell   Yes, of course.

Wedgecroft, *on the point of leaving, feels he must be just to* **Horsham**, *who had – though so unwittingly – angered him a little.*

Wedgecroft   Horsham blamed himself bitterly . . . and he i s very, very upset. Dear Frances . . . you've pluck enough for twenty.

Frances Trebell   No. I'm stunned. I shall come round . . .
and it'll hurt . . . and I still want it to. Then I shall wonder
why he did it. Now I know . . . glimmeringly.

Wedgecroft   Do you?

Frances Trebell   Why . . . when you come to think of it,
Gilbert . . . life, for its own sake, is an overrated thing.

Wedgecroft, *who will not play the professional comforter, says no more
but goes. As he passes* **Walter** *emerging from his room the two exchange
British greetings.*

Wedgecroft   Hullo.

Walter Kent   Hullo.

Walter *has some papers in his hand which he is bringing without much
thinking why, to put on* **Trebell**'s *table. He is undisguisedly crying. He
sees* **Frances** *sitting there, silent, still. He gulps out . . .*

Walter Kent   Selfish of me to make a fool of myself before
you!

Frances Trebell   No, Walter, no . . . I'll cry when I can.

Walter Kent   I'm not grieving . . . I'm angry. I don't want
to whisper and hide things. I'd like go through the streets and
shout that he's dead . . . that they've lost him and wasted him,
damn them! With his work all undone! Who's to do it? Much
they care! What did they know of him? We knew. I cared.
I was nothing to him . . . but I cared. That's waste too. What
does it matter? Oh, the waste of him . . . oh, the waste . . .
the waste!

But this is very foolish, and quite useless.

 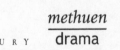

Bloomsbury Methuen Drama Modern Plays
include work by

Bola Agbaje
Edward Albee
Davey Anderson
Jean Anouilh
John Arden
Peter Barnes
Sebastian Barry
Alistair Beaton
Brendan Behan
Edward Bond
William Boyd
Bertolt Brecht
Howard Brenton
Amelia Bullmore
Anthony Burgess
Leo Butler
Jim Cartwright
Lolita Chakrabarti
Caryl Churchill
Lucinda Coxon
Curious Directive
Nick Darke
Shelagh Delaney
Ishy Din
Claire Dowie
David Edgar
David Eldridge
Dario Fo
Michael Frayn
John Godber
Paul Godfrey
James Graham
David Greig
John Guare
Mark Haddon
Peter Handke
David Harrower
Jonathan Harvey
Iain Heggie

Robert Holman
Caroline Horton
Terry Johnson
Sarah Kane
Barrie Keeffe
Doug Lucie
Anders Lustgarten
David Mamet
Patrick Marber
Martin McDonagh
Arthur Miller
D. C. Moore
Tom Murphy
Phyllis Nagy
Anthony Neilson
Peter Nichols
Joe Orton
Joe Penhall
Luigi Pirandello
Stephen Poliakoff
Lucy Prebble
Peter Quilter
Mark Ravenhill
Philip Ridley
Willy Russell
Jean-Paul Sartre
Sam Shepard
Martin Sherman
Wole Soyinka
Simon Stephens
Peter Straughan
Kate Tempest
Theatre Workshop
Judy Upton
Timberlake Wertenbaker
Roy Williams
Snoo Wilson
Frances Ya-Chu Cowhig
Benjamin Zephaniah

Bloomsbury Methuen Drama Contemporary Dramatists

include

John Arden (two volumes)
Arden & D'Arcy
Peter Barnes (three volumes)
Sebastian Barry
Mike Bartlett
Dermot Bolger
Edward Bond (eight volumes)
Howard Brenton (two volumes)
Leo Butler
Richard Cameron
Jim Cartwright
Caryl Churchill (two volumes)
Complicite
Sarah Daniels (two volumes)
Nick Darke
David Edgar (three volumes)
David Eldridge (two volumes)
Ben Elton
Per Olov Enquist
Dario Fo (two volumes)
Michael Frayn (four volumes)
John Godber (four volumes)
Paul Godfrey
James Graham
David Greig
John Guare
Lee Hall (two volumes)
Katori Hall
Peter Handke
Jonathan Harvey (two volumes)
Iain Heggie
Israel Horovitz
Declan Hughes
Terry Johnson (three volumes)
Sarah Kane
Barrie Keeffe
Bernard-Marie Koltès (two volumes)
Franz Xaver Kroetz
Kwame Kwei-Armah
David Lan
Bryony Lavery
Deborah Levy
Doug Lucie

David Mamet (four volumes)
Patrick Marber
Martin McDonagh
Duncan McLean
David Mercer (two volumes)
Anthony Minghella (two volumes)
Tom Murphy (six volumes)
Phyllis Nagy
Anthony Neilson (two volumes)
Peter Nichol (two volumes)
Philip Osment
Gary Owen
Louise Page
Stewart Parker (two volumes)
Joe Penhall (two volumes)
Stephen Poliakoff (three volumes)
David Rabe (two volumes)
Mark Ravenhill (three volumes)
Christina Reid
Philip Ridley (two volumes)
Willy Russell
Eric-Emmanuel Schmitt
Ntozake Shange
Sam Shepard (two volumes)
Martin Sherman (two volumes)
Christopher Shinn
Joshua Sobel
Wole Soyinka (two volumes)
Simon Stephens (three volumes)
Shelagh Stephenson
David Storey (three volumes)
C. P. Taylor
Sue Townsend
Judy Upton
Michel Vinaver (two volumes)
Arnold Wesker (two volumes)
Peter Whelan
Michael Wilcox
Roy Williams (four volumes)
David Williamson
Snoo Wilson (two volumes)
David Wood (two volumes)
Victoria Wood

For a complete listing of Bloomsbury
Methuen Drama titles, visit:
www.bloomsbury.com/drama

Follow us on Twitter and keep up to date
with our news and publications
@MethuenDrama